RUTH SALVAGGIO

Dryden's Dualities

ELS
EDITIONS

ELS Editions
Department of English
University of Victoria
Victoria, BC
Canada V8W 3W1
www.elseditions.com

Founding Editor: Samuel L. Macey

General Editor: Luke Carson

Printed by CreateSpace

English literary studies monograph series
ISSN 0829-7681 ; 29
ISBN-10 0-920604-11-0
ISBN-13 978-0-920604-11-3

*This is for my mother,
and in memory of my father.*

CONTENTS

Preface   7

1. The Double Poet, His "Double Beat"   11

2. Dryden and Notions of Duality   26

3. Duality as Structure: The Divided Worlds of *All For Love*   43

4. Duality as Politics: Doubletalk in *Absalom and Achitophel*   60

5. Duality as Dismissal: The Uncertainties of *Religio Laici*   79

Afterword: Dividing the Crown   94

Notes   98

PREFACE

There is nothing unusual about finding double structures in Dryden. He loved debate and discourse, and his closed couplet verse naturally lent itself to parallels and juxtapositions of language. But there has also been a very traditional way of explaining the presence of these double structures. Normally we see Dryden adopting a position somewhere in the middle of his arguments--reflecting compromise and balance in his final position. Either/or exclusions become both/and resolutions, with Dryden as spokesman for the moderate middle position. And we see him weaving his poetic language--despite the fact that it often relies on paradox and opposition--into a final synthesis, a firm statement.

My study of Dryden's dualities questions these assumptions, and suggests instead that the double structures we find in Dryden go deeper than the outlines of his arguments or the superficial dialectic of his language. I try to show that Dryden's poetic vision is remarkably dualistic, that the double structures we find in his works are characteristic of a writer who loved to engage himself in the two-sidedness of literary subjects. Unlike the "mighty opposites" of Shakespeare or the paradoxes of Donne, Dryden's dualities seem to me more like those of the duelist who enjoys the art of duelling. Over and over again, I have found the liveliest parts of Dryden's works to be those where divisions become most extreme, where he can exploit their poetic possibilities. In tracing dualities in both the man and his works, I argue that it is impossible to form a critical estimation of Dryden without taking into account the interplay involved in his dualistic vision.

What follows in the text of this study is both a framework for approaching dualities in Dryden and an analysis of dualities in his works. I have found it useful to investigate biographical and historical context to remind us of the duplicities inherent in Dryden's character and his age--duplicities which we have tended to overlook in our search for the true nature of the man and a sense of coherency about the times in which he lived. I have also found it useful to define a context for dualities in specific works by indicating how dualities function in that work--for dramatic structure, political doubletalk, and religious debate. And finally, I have found it useful to apply some contemporary critical theories to my reading of Dryden's text, theories which offer yet another context for my study, and which show Dryden to be a writer just as receptive to distinctly modern critical perspectives as he has been in the past to the criticism of such figures as Samuel Johnson, Walter Scott, and T.S. Eliot.

A word remains to be said about my choice of texts. Quite simply, I have selected three works which in many ways represent Dryden's great literary achievements. *All For Love* is the world of drama, but it is also a world of character interaction, debated ideas, and heroic style. In *Absalom and Achitophel* there is the world of politics and history, but also of epic and narrative verse, caricature, and couplet satire. *Religio Laici* is the world of religious systems, of theological controversy and couplet discourse. In a sense, what Dryden writes about and how he writes in these literary works reveal much that is germane to all of his poetry. Of course I have had another principle in mind when approaching my study. I have looked for works which best exemplify the literary process of doubling and division, and have organized my analysis around specific kinds of duality--structural, political, and theological-- which frame the analysis of duality within the concerns of a specific text.

Two poems which receive comparatively limited criticism in this study are actually more ₁ .votal than my treatment of them might indicate. I use the St. Cecilia's Day odes to introduce the subject of discovering dualities in the text, and return to them in the "Afterword" for a second view of their dualities--and for a final view of Dryden's dualities. Both poems appeared well after the three major works which I discuss. And because the odes are a purer form of poetry--lyrical celebration--I use them to show the pure aesthetic appeal of Dryden's dualistic vision which allows him to engage in his own feast of oppositions.

* * *

Most criticism grows out of other criticism, and a student of Dryden fortunately inherits a rich critical tradition. As it turns out, I think that several fine Shakespeare scholars have also influenced me, notably in my attempt to describe dualistic structures in literary expression. Reference to all these critics in the notes often only begins to acknowledge my scholarly debts.

During the past five years I have exchanged ideas about Dryden and poetry and criticism with many friends and colleagues, particularly those at Rice University and Virginia Polytechnic Institute. I have learned something from every one of them. I'm especially glad that I began my study of Dryden with William Bowman Piper, who was still reading and commenting on the manuscript in its final stages.

A NOTE ON THE TEXT

References to *Absalom and Achitophel* and *Religio Laici* are to *The Works of John Dryden*, ed. H.T. Swedenberg, Jr. and Vinton A. Dearing (Berkeley: Univ. of Calif. Press, 1972), II, and are noted throughout by line number. References to *All For Love* are to David M. Vieth's edition of the play, Regents Restoration Drama Series (Lincoln: Univ. of Nebraska Press, 1972), which cites line numbers. My citations are by act and line number. Of the other Dryden poems that I treat, some have and some have not yet appeared in the California Dryden. For convenience, then, these references are to *The Poems of John Dryden*, ed. James Kinsley, 4 vols. (Oxford: Clarendon, 1958), and are cited by line number.

CHAPTER 1

The Double Poet,
His "Double Beat"

In 1662, when Dryden was just beginning his poetic career, he composed a poem entitled "To my Honour'd Friend, Dr. Charleton." The date is significant for two reasons: it marks the beginning of Dryden's brief but consequential association with the Royal Society, and it also marks the time during which he wrote his first poems in praise of the restored King Charles.[1] In the epistle, Dryden manages to address both these subjects. Both Charleton and Charles, for instance, are the subject of a restoration--Charleton's restoration of Stonehenge to its true founders, and the restoration of Charles himself to the throne of England. The issue becomes more divided when we realize that the epistle revolves around two other subjects--science and politics. The question finally arises as to what the poem is really about: Charleton and science, or Charles and politics.

It is a question on which criticism itself is divided. If we follow the arguments of this criticism, then we must necessarily believe that the poem is about *either* Charleton *or* Charles. Moreover, each critical perspective accounts for the dual thrusts of the poem in different ways. According to the view that the poem is ultimately about Charles, for instance, Dryden contrasts political metaphor and scientific subject in the opening lines in order to enforce parallels between scientific and political figures, such as Aristotle and Cromwell, or Columbus and General Monck. According to the view that the poem is about Charleton, Dryden is actually employing "encomiastic analogy" in order to enhance his praise of Charleton by comparing him to the more famous scientists of the day, and ultimately to Columbus. Thus we end up with two diametrically opposed viewpoints. One holds that "the ultimate objective of the epistle is to celebrate the Stuart reign"; the other insists that "the subject remains throughout Charleton and his book, for which Dryden is free to find more than one means of praise."[2]

What I find interesting about the epistle to Charleton is not simply that it possesses a double subject, but that it is permeated with double structures. In addition to comparing individuals and contrasting metaphor and subject, Dryden frames several of his statements around pairs of opposites. He tells of Columbus, for instance, discovering "a

11

Temp'rate in a *Torrid* Zone" where "the *fevrish aire*" is "fann'd by a cooling breez." He ascribes to Bacon not only the world's *"present* Knowledge, but its *future* too." He contrasts the belief that Stonehenge was a *"Temple"* with Charleton's theory that it was a *"Throne."*

Yet another kind of dual structuring in the poem is that which also underlies the spirit of scientific investigation. Instead of deriving truth from the logical progression of ideas, scientists more often sought truth through the awareness of previous errors. Thus Dryden writes to Charleton:

> What ever *Truths* have been, by *Art* or *Chance*,
> Redeem'd from *Error*, or from *Ignorance*,
> Thin in their *Authors*, (like rich veins of Ore)
> Your Works unite, and still discover more.

On two occasions Dryden provides specific examples of this truth-error dichotomy: first, Harvey's theory of the circulation of the blood--

> The *Circling* streams, once thought but pools, of blood
> (Whether Life's fewel, or the Bodie's food)
> From dark Oblivion *Harvey's* name shall save;

and then Charleton's hypothesis about Stonehenge--

> STONE-HENG, once thought a *Temple*, You have found
> A *Throne*, where Kings, our Earthly Gods, were Crown'd.

We can extend this sort of duality which involves the opposition of truth and error to include an even larger notion of duality in the epistle, the notion that any single truth is automatically suspect because without contrary ideas we cannot discover what truth is. The very opening lines of the poem, for instance, describe the tyranny of Aristotelian dogmatism, a *"Truth"* which is tyrannical because it is not questioned. Such truth, Dryden says, "while onely one suppli'd the State, / Grew scarce...." Thus Columbus, who is the first to shake Aristotle's "Throne," discovers the exact opposite of what would be expected: a temperate in a torrid zone, a cooling breeze fanning the feverish air. The dominance of one truth is not only foreign to the spirit of science, as Dryden describes it here, but foreign to Dryden's own thought process, at least in this poem, where he relies on two kinds of truth--original and revised--for his praise of Charleton.

If the epistle to Charleton, then, has two distinct subjects, we can also say that it contains a variety of other double structures. We might say that it is a severely divided poem. But the double structures and themes we find in it--analogies and parallels, juxtapositions and oppositions, even philosophical dialectic--are all quite characteristic of Dryden. They are

12

his dualities. They manifest themselves in different ways in different works, but their basic design is always present. They are not only characteristic of Dryden's poetic technique, but a characteristic way of his thinking and writing.

What I propose is an examination of these dualities--in the poet himself, in his intellectual context, and most importantly in his works. In doing so, I will be questioning our dominant impression of Dryden as a writer possessed of a single, well-integrated character, and will suggest instead that he is a remarkably two-sided figure who exploits the poetic tension of dual structures. We can find evidence of the interplay of these dual structures everywhere in his works. But that is because we can find them first in the man himself--a writer clearly divided in his own personal outlook and poetic practice. Before discussing the contextual and literary nature of Dryden's dualities, then, I want first to explore this double poet and his "double beat."

The Double Poet

John Dryden is a poet who has left us with a firm impression of his character, despite the fact that we have so little direct information about his life. Several assumptions about him have become ingrained in our perspective: we see him as a very public figure, a respected critic, a popular dramatist, and apparently a strong supporter of the conservative cause in politics and religion. But there has also been another side to Dryden, an aspect of his character captured by all of his biographers--not Dryden as a man consumed with the defense of strict political and moral positions, but rather as a man himself consumed by the variety and range of issues in Restoration England. Samuel Johnson was surely alluding to such a quality when he described Dryden's willingness to engage in dual sides of issues:

> The favorite exercise of his mind was ratiocination....
> When once he had engaged himself in disputation,
> thoughts flowed in on either side: he was now no longer at a
> loss; he had always objections and solutions at command:
> 'verbaque provisam rem'--give him matter for his verse, and
> he finds without difficulty verse for his matter.[3]

Dryden's predilection to have thoughts flow in "on either side" has been a constant source of trouble for many of his biographers and critics. Sir Walter Scott blatantly admitted that when it came to dealing with Dryden's conversion to Catholicism shortly after the ascension of James II, "the biographer of Dryden must feel considerable difficulty in discussing the probable causes of his change."[4] And although George Saintsbury carefully discriminated Dryden's motives in changing his

13

political and religious opinions, finally vouching for the poet's sincerity, he nonetheless admitted a certain amount of "unconscious insincerity" on Dryden's part, concluding:

> If I judge his character aright, no English man of letters was ever more thoroughly susceptible to the spirit and influence of his time. Dryden was essentially a literary man, and was disposed rather to throw himself into the arms of any party than into those of one so hopelessly unliterary as the ultra-liberal and ultra-Protestant party of the seventeenth century was. He was moreover a professed servant of the public, or as we should put it in these days, he had the journalistic spirit.[5]

Here is the picture of the "other" Dryden, an uncomfortable picture: though it praises the man for his openness of spirit and willingness to be a flexible public spokesman, it calls into question the sincerity of his motives. To borrow Saintsbury's phrase, "in these days" the same questions are as unsettling and disturbing to critics. We somehow feel more comfortable with the notion of Dryden as a defender of the "conservative myth," or the belief that he was after all a deeply religious Anglican. There is a long history to these confirmed assumptions. But there is an equally demanding history to the biography and criticism which discovers another Dryden altogether, a character who leaves us feeling somewhat unsure about what he is saying, yet one far more interesting and dynamic as an artist. Let me sketch the main outlines of this perspective.

The "other" Dryden has traditionally been portrayed as a turncoat, an individual who switched his loyalties and opinions in order to gain favor with the party in power. Though such a portrait has now been almost totally erased, it was by no means strictly the product of what James Osborn labeled "the picture of the inconsistent turncoat so cherished by Whiggish writers for two centuries after his death...."[6] Dryden had an enormous number of enemies among his own seventeenth-century contemporaries who typically accused him, at one point or another, of being two-faced. Particularly the lampoons written after the publication of *Absalom and Achitophel* evidence the lash of such contemporary criticism. Scott notes the case of one "incensed antagonist" who, disturbed by the inconsistency of Dryden's eulogy on Cromwell and his ensuing support of Charles, entitled his attack "An Elegy on the Usurper O.C., by the author of Absalom and Achitophel, published ... to show the loyalty and integrity of the poet."[7] Such sarcasm is typical of the attacks, and Dryden himself gives us some indication of their popularity when he admitted that "More libels have been written against me, than almost any Man now living."[8] It should come as no surprise, then, that all of Dryden's biographers have devoted substantial discussion to the question of his sincerity.

Even the earliest biographies address the issue. Thomas Birch's account of Dryden, which appeared in Bayle's *General Dictionary, Historical and Critical* in 1736, quotes one estimation of the poet that describes the "inconstancy of his temper" which "mixed with the conduct of his writings, as well as his life."[9] Such comments were typical in the eighteenth-century biographies of Dryden. Samuel Derrick found it necessary to defend him against accusations of being "a time-server and hypocrite in religion," and Edmond Malone, whose thorough and extensive account of Dryden's life was published in 1800, devoted substantial discussion to the political and religious attacks directed against him.[10] This traditional defense of Dryden usually relied on either a direct rebuttal of the attacks or an explanation of how Dryden's "temper" or personality affected the often contradictory nature of his discourse. Though both lines of defense can be found in the major accounts of Dryden, it is the latter of the two--the description of his personal nature--that attracted the attention of his great literary biographers.

We might consider, for instance, Johnson's almost casual commentary on Dryden's political changes: "If he changed, he changed with the nation."[11] Or take Johnson's remarks on Dryden's religious instability:

> If men of argument and study can find such difficulties or such motives, as may either unite them to the church of Rome or detain them in uncertainty, there can be no wonder that a man, who perhaps never enquired why he was a protestant, should by an artful and experienced disputant be made a papist, overborne by the sudden violence of new and unexpected arguments, or deceived by a representation which shews only the doubts on one part and only the evidence on the other.[12]

With these remarks, we are clearly back into Johnson's sketch of the two-sided Dryden, an individual easily lured by the influence of both sides of issues, apparently for the very reason that such a dialectic came so naturally to him. Johnson is clearly focusing attention on Dryden's own personal inclinations. But he is also indicating something else. By suggesting that Dryden was responsive to current trends in politics or to persuasive argument in religion, he is reminding us of something that we have come to recognize as one of Dryden's distinctive qualities--that he was a man of his age, a person always embroiled in every controversy, always involved in the latest events. Scott considered this responsiveness to public opinion to be in fact a sort of dependence on it, claiming that

Dryden was after all a poet who "wrote from necessity ... obliged to pay a certain deference to the public opinion ... so that he alternately influenced and stooped to the national taste of the day."[13] Scott himself had no less an ambition in his *Life of Dryden* than to uncover "how far the age was indebted to the poet, and how far the poet was influenced by the taste and manners of the age." And Scott's conclusion about the character of Dryden suggests, as had Johnson's observations, that such give-and-take between poet and community nicely coincided with the flexible and dexterous cast of Dryden's mind which, according to Scott, was prone "to entangle itself in sophistical toils of its own weaving.... His opinions, doubtless, are often inconsistent, and sometimes absolutely contradictory.... His arguments, even in the worst cause, bear witness to the energy of his mental conceptions."[14]

Similar explanations for Dryden's mental flexibility can be found in Saintsbury's early twentieth-century biography. In answering the accusations of Macaulay, for instance, Saintsbury poses just the right questions about political expediency and the influence of social circumstance, asking that if Macaulay had been presented with "an equal opening when he was a young man for distinction and profit as a Tory, for early retirement on literary pursuits with a competence, and for all the other things which he most desired, is it quite so certain that he would not have been of the other persuasion?"[15] And like both Johnson and Scott, Saintsbury was impressed with the fluid and sometimes shifty cast of Dryden's mind. In commenting on Dryden's "singular faculty of verse argument," he writes:

> But Dryden's didactic poems are quite unlike anything which came before them, and have never been approached by anything that has come after them. Doubtless they prove nothing ... but at the same time they have a remarkable air of proving something.... The bent of his mind, moreover, was of that peculiar kind which delights in arguing a point. Something of this may be traced in the singular variety, not to say inconsistency, even of his literary judgments. He sees, for the time being, only the point which he has set himself to prove, and is quite careless of the fact that he has proved something very different yesterday, and is very likely to prove something different still to-morrow.[16]

For nearly three centuries Dryden's biographers were, I think, unconsciously responding to a double poet. On the one hand, to them Dryden was a poet with a well-defined personality and well-defined themes; on the other hand, he was a chameleon figure momentarily caught up in different issues and swayed by different sides of argument. But the double picture simply would not hold together. Particularly after the assaults on Dryden made during the nineteenth century, it seemed more necessary than ever to lay the chameleon figure to rest. Not surprisingly, we find James Osborn and Charles Ward emphatically dismissing the issue of Dryden's inconstancy and insincerity. Their assumptions are remarkably in tune with the major assumptions of modern Dryden criticism, which considers the "chameleon Dryden" to be a mistaken characterization which has unfortunately crept into our historical estimation of the poet. When Osborn, for instance, discusses Christie's accusations against Dryden, he focuses attention on Christie's partisan motives, lamenting the fact that so biased a figure "probably has done more harm to Dryden's reputation than any other biographer."[17] Ward seems singularly anxious, and again justifiably so, to end once and for all the smear campaign against Dryden. When commenting on the political philosophy Dryden voices in *Absalom and Achitophel,* he concludes: "Dryden was no Trimmer: he had taken his stand on an hereditary Monarchy bound by law and by a Parliament of the two houses; and looking back with a 'wise affright,' he had rejected the commonwealth principle of a supreme Parliament. So far as can be determined he never changed."[18] With this same settled conviction, Ward explains Dryden's switch to Catholicism: "That Dryden's conversion came as the result of a long and sincere quest for answers to his religious doubts seems clear."[19] Modern Dryden scholars have rooted their criticism in this picture of the unified Dryden, a picture which has survived after three centuries of debate over who the real Dryden actually is. Now that issue seems to be settled. Today we find Dryden critics addressing consistent themes; we find them analyzing consistent aspects of style.

Surely the paradoxical result of attempts made by Dryden's biographers to explain his apparent inconsistencies is that their greatest insights have become cliche. We now take for granted that Dryden had a "large" mind and an "enormous range" as a poet, yet we have never credited him with a vision any wider than the confines of the conservative positions which he seemed to support. Somewhat ironically, then, our picture of him as one of the most complexly involved and conspicuous figures of his age has taken second place to our firmer and more settled notion of Dryden as the voice of conservatism in Restoration England. Modern criticism is rich in its observations about Dryden's poetic achievement, but in ignoring some of the best insights of Johnson, Scott, and Saintsbury, in accepting once and for all the picture of the unified Dryden, it has been notably one-sided.

Recently, for instance, Harold Love called attention to a kind of paradoxical and incoherent conceit that was typical of Dryden, a conceit which Samuel Johnson labeled as the poet's "unideal vacancy," his delight "to tread upon the brink of meaning, where light and darkness begin to mingle...." In addressing Johnson's remarks, Love makes a particularly revealing observation about the ways in which we have come to understand Dryden: "This," he says, "is emphatically not the Dryden of twentieth-century criticism."[20] Love's analysis, to which I will devote more attention later, turns over some of our long-held assumptions about Dryden's poetry, and presents us with a figure strikingly different from the individual we are used to seeing. But why have we not before recognized Dryden's fondness for contradiction and paradox? Let me quote Love's explanation:

> Our situation has been much like that of the four sentinels in the Chesterton story who fail to observe the murderer because he is disguised as a postman. The difference is that in Dryden's case we fail to see anything except postmen, functional, informative, unshowy creatures. It is the extravagantly dressed dandy who escapes our observation.[21]

Twentieth-century Dryden critics to a large extent have sought the plain and unshowy in the midst of the extravagant. A statement of Mark Van Doren's comes to mind: "When Dryden became fired he only wrote more plainly."[22]

In a sense, Van Doren's assumptions have governed the development of modern Dryden scholarship. We have tamed Dryden--accounted for his inconsistencies, explained his "conservative myth" and "poetic kingdoms," identified his "milieu," his religious "contexts" and his "traditions," analyzed the "art" and "craft" of his style, his "imagery."[23] When Paul Ramsey wrote, with reference to *Absalom and Achitophel*, that Dryden's "bedrock method of satire and panegyric, underlying all the range and clustering of brilliant technique, is simply statement and argument,"[24] he was drawing on a very traditional and firmly entrenched attitude about the poet. We are constantly reminding ourselves not to get carried away in our observations, to remember that Dryden was after all a reasonable man. And we have refused to admit--as some of his biographers likely would not--that Dryden might indeed have moved beyond the point that Johnson called "the brink of meaning."

I am suggesting that we can afford to make such an admission. I am also suggesting that we should question some of our basic assumptions about the kind of poet Dryden was--one who made statements and arguments and who, though he might have enjoyed debating both sides of issues, always presented a well-defined case, a conclusion, a theme. For I think we can see from his great literary biographers that such was not Dryden's own nature, and I think we can see from some of the intellectual trends of his day that such was not the nature of seventeenth-century

England. An article which in many ways summarizes what I have been referring to as the "unified Dryden" is Thomas Fujimura's "The Temper of John Dryden." His depiction is interesting because it moves in two directions. On the one hand he sees Dryden as "vigorous, aggressive, and independent," a poet who relied on imagery of "combat and struggle in the literary, political, and religious arenas," who had a "predilection for the forensic mode." Yet Fujimura believes that in the very vigor of Dryden's combat and debate, he was expressing "a fundamental attitude and oneness of thought and temper." Dryden's "strong character," he concludes, "leaves an indelible impression of a vital, integrated person, who speaks clearly in all his works, and who moves us by virtue of his particular integrity."[25] To this argument, I would pose one basic question: would it not be more reasonable to believe that a poet so consumed with the division and clash of issues is in fact not an "integrated person" at all, but one ultimately torn between the dual structures which he himself continually creates?

This alternate assumption obviously postulates that Dryden was a double poet--not only in the sense that his biographers and critics have tended to view him in two different ways, but also in the sense that he himself was consumed with double subjects and dual forms of expression. Such a depiction of Dryden is radically different from our traditional picture of him, yet it is a perspective that has engaged the thought of at least a few notable critics and scholars. I would like to examine briefly four different critical perspectives on the double Dryden, each of which departs from traditional assumptions and helps, I think, to define a long overdue revaluation of his character and his poetry.

The first dates back to 1930, and was so tenuous that its author dismissed some of the most insightful implications of his own argument. I am referring to William Empson's brief analysis of Dryden's verse form in his *Seven Types of Ambiguity*.[26] Empson identified a double movement in Dryden's verse--the backward and forward reference of his syntax, a feature of style that he also found characteristic of Shakespeare. But he begins his analysis with notable hesitancy: "It is interesting to find Dryden," he writes, "using the sort of ambiguity of syntax we have considered in the Shakespeare Sonnets, which, on the whole, is not encouraged by the couplet." As an example, he quotes these lines from Dryden's translation of Boccaccio:

> And what to *Guiscard* is already done,
> Or to be done, is doom'd by thy Decree.

Empson explains the ambiguity: *"Or to be done* conveys 'is to be done to Guiscard,' or 'is doomed to be done by thy decree,' going with the phrase before or after...."[27] Yet the ambiguity still seems to him somehow out of

19

place in Dryden, "on the whole, not encouraged by the couplet." He even suggests that had someone pointed out to Dryden the dual thrust of his syntax, the poet might have altered it--though his suspicion lingers that Dryden would have felt such a change to be "a pity." Empson is not the only reader of Dryden to observe his slippery syntax,[28] but he is, I think, the only one to entertain the possibility that Dryden--almost in spite of himself and in spite of the stylistic standards of his age--actually might have approved of the technique. In this sense Empson's insights were ignored by Dryden critics: stylistic ambiguity was not to be a quality associated with this poet.

A very different approach to the notion of duality in Dryden was offered by Edward Pechter in his study of *Dryden's Classical Theory of Literature* which appeared in 1975. In examining the flexibility of Dryden's critical ideas, ideas that allowed Dryden to perceive "literary qualities in terms of complementaries--both/and," Pechter argues that Dryden was adopting a "classical" stance. In his admiration for both French and English drama, for instance, or in the complementary arguments presented in *An Essay of Dramatic Poesy*, or in his balanced comparison of Horace and Juvenal, Dryden--according to Pechter--is following the "classical mean" which "describes a dynamic balance between different kinds of values."[29] The consistent presence of this balance in Dryden's critical theory is what Pechter refers to as Dryden's "doubleness."

I find Pechter's arguments particularly relevant to my own ideas because he is the first to apply positively the notion of "doubleness" to any of Dryden's works. Yet in adopting such a traditionally positive explanation for the doubleness, Pechter may also be narrowing the implications of his insights. One cannot help but entertain the possibility--especially in light of the shifty cast of Dryden's mind--that there might be an explanation other than that of the classical mean to account for the doubleness of Dryden.

This possibility obviously brings us to a consideration of Dryden's own poetic thought, a subject which Irvin Ehrenpreis addressed in his Clark Lecture on Dryden in 1974, "Continuity and Coruscation: Dryden's Poetic Instincts." What Ehrenpreis suggests is that we can find a basic "discontinuity" of genre and style in Dryden, as in *Alexander's Feast*, for instance, where Dryden merges the sublimity of the old Pindaric ode with the tone of "a cheerful drinking song, smelling, as Landor said, of gin."[30] To Ehrenpreis, this "literary habit probably reflects a deeper instinct of Dryden's mind," one that allowed him not only to engage but actually support both sides of issues, a habit that Ehrenpreis calls Dryden's "essentially dualistic genius."[31] His assumptions differ from Pechter's in

20

that they focus on Dryden himself rather than on a critical tradition which he followed. Indeed I cannot help but see Ehrenpreis's suggestions as the corollary to those of Fujimura, each critic identifying a radically different basis of Dryden's instinct and temper.

The relevance of Ehrenpreis's observations to my argument should be obvious. By focusing attention on Dryden's own "instincts," he takes us back to the biographical explorations of the poet's cast of mind. And in suggesting that Dryden possessed a dualistic frame of thought, one that would at least account for the discontinuities of genre and style, he unfolds a very different portrait of Dryden--different at least to our critical sensibility, but not foreign to Johnson, Scott, and Saintsbury, however tenuously they articulated their discoveries.

With these perspectives in mind, I can now return to Harold Love's discussion of "Dryden's Unideal Vacancy" which extends such explorations into the character of the poet. Love is not hesitant to admit that Dryden's "brilliant incoherencies" and his delight in "paradox" and "contradiction" are inherent in his very thought, that they characterize "the extravagantly dressed dandy" who has consistently escaped our attention. The nature of these incoherencies, Love explains, is expressed in terms of "a collision of irreconcilable conceptions" that may involve a variety of oppositions. Though Love typically focuses on incoherencies of specific conceits and images, he also discusses "kinds of disparity" which "reflect the wider philosophical dilemmas of the Restoration poet...."[32] He even offers Dryden's depiction of Charles in *Absalom and Achitophel* as an example of such a collision of ideas: "that of the pagan libertine of the opening lines with the sanctified king who delivers God's judgment at the close."[33] Clearly such a duality would point not only to Dryden's own delight in his contradictory portrait of Charles, but the delight his readers could take in such a portrait as well. Johnson's term "delight" is in fact the give-away word, for in using this term Love has added--or, more accurately, rediscovered--the most vital dimension to the context for Dryden's dualities: Dryden not only could find them in tune with his own instincts, but he could enjoy them, indeed exploit them, as an artist. If, as Love suggests, this is not the Dryden of twentieth-century criticism, then we might say, borrowing Empson's terms, that it is a pity. For the richness of Dryden's art owes much to both the casual play and the powerful tension of his dualities.[34]

The Double Beat

My discussion has thus far been biographical; I have spoken *about* Dryden. Before proceeding to an examination of his intellectual background where I think we can uncover several notions of duality that

21

help account for Dryden's own double nature, I would like to address some of his works directly. The major problem in making this transition is that it is difficult to describe in any simple way the dimension of Dryden's dualities. And yet without some sense of how they manifest themselves, of how they work in his poetry, it would be impossible to come to grips with the dualities as characteristic of Dryden's literary personality, his age, or his art. Let me suggest, then, that a good way to begin is to look closely at a couple of his poems. I have already devoted some attention to one of Dryden's very early poems, his epistle to Charleton. We can turn now to some late poems, surely also some of his most famous--the St. Cecilia's Day odes.

When Dryden was commissioned to write the St. Cecilia's Day odes, he was also becoming part of a long tradition in poetry--inheriting not only the popular subjects for the odes, but structures, images, and metaphors as well.[35] Yet at the same time he stamped his contribution to this tradition in a peculiar fashion that owes very little to his predecessors. Dryden's poems are not ultimately about St. Cecilia, who more properly serves as the "occasion" for the odes. Nor do they celebrate the power of music, a point which several critics have recently debated.[36] Instead, I think that Dryden used the beat of music to convey a much more powerful theme for him--the force of opposites. We can discover the framework for these oppositions in "A Song for St. Cecilia's Day." Music first brings harmony to the universe, uniting the "jarring Atomes" into pairs--"cold, and hot, and moist, and dry," until the "Diapason" is seen as "closing full in Man." But the end of the poem wrenches these pairs apart. The "heav'nly Harmony" of the first stanza is upset as an angel, hearing the music of the organ, mistakes "Earth for Heaven." In the final "Grand CHORUS," the world is inverted. *"This crumbling Pagaent"* is devoured by time: *"The Dead shall live, the Living die, / And MUSICK shall untune the sky."* We begin with harmony, with "This universal Frame." We end with untuning, with *"This crumbling Pagaent."* And we move from beginning to end through a series of double beats.

The poem is in fact saturated with dualities of structure and language and subject. "What Passion cannot MUSICK raise and quell!" opens and closes the second stanza. In the very same way that harmony and disharmony provide a dualistic structure for the ode, so the raising and quelling of passion structures smaller units within the poem, and at the same time rocks us back and forth between the heights of emotion and silences of rest. First there is the thunder of war, "The double double double beat / Of the thundring DRUM." And there are oppositions of movement within the very battle scene: "The Foes come ... 'tis too late to retreat." But then there is the softness of woe, where movement hardly exists but for the "warbling" vibration of the lute. Finally we encounter the frenzy of jealousy, an emotion itself built on irreconcilable opposed feelings--"Depth of Pains, and height of Passion, / For the fair, disdainful Dame."

One would expect the arrival of St. Cecilia and her organ music to be some unifying force, recalling the "Diapason" and "heav'nly Harmony" of the opening stanza. And yet these "Notes that wing their heav'nly ways / To mend the Choires above" have just the opposite effect. Cecilia becomes a higher form of Orpheus, her prototype in classical myth, enticing an uncontrolled lust for her music. Thus the "Trees unrooted left their place" enamoured of Orpheus's spell, and an angel, in like fashion, mistakes earth for heaven upon hearing Cecilia's "vocal Breath."

Of course what I have just suggested is one way of reading the poem. Another possibility is that Cecilia does indeed bring harmony into the world, and that the angel mistakes earth for heaven for the very reason that Cecilia has brought a kind of "heav'nly Harmony" to this world. And I am at least willing to entertain this possibility because I think it reflects *one* of Dryden's subjects--the traditional praise of St. Cecilia. But such a reading does not take into account the disharmony of the grand chorus which ends the ode, a chorus which returns to the double beat of the trumpet and drum, of war, of the savage race that Orpheus led. For this is Dryden's *other* subject. Considering the two subjects, it is impossible to say exactly what his theme is. Like the epistle to Charleton, but in a more profound sense, "A Song for St. Cecilia's Day" celebrates a series of two different subjects: heaven and earth, Cecilia and Orpheus, and the drastically opposed musical tones that enforce harmony and disharmony. I would suggest that Dryden himself is entangled in the dual structures, that he is the one who mistakes earth for heaven, at least in the sense that the two forces which vie for his support cannot distinguish themselves as one superior to the other. We will often find Dryden in this captive position; he is often caught between what his poems should be about and what they are in fact about. Moreover, he is caught between antithetical modes of expression dictated by these disparate poetic schemes.

We can see these oppositions manifesting themselves in a more complicated fashion in *Alexander's Feast*, Dryden's other ode in honor of St. Cecilia's day, written ten years after the first. It would be nearly impossible to say what the ode is singularly about. If it is about Cecilia, it devotes all of its energy to the master musician Timotheus. If it is about the power of music to excite passion, then which passion? If it is about Alexander's "Feast," then what exactly is that feast?

In the opening lines of the poem we find the warlike Alexander on his throne, with the lovely Thais by his side. They are apparently the

"Happy Pair"--one brave, one fair. And yet the poem really provides us with a series of paired figures: Jove and Olympia, Bacchus and Darius, Timotheus and Cecilia. In each we find diametrically opposed characteristics. When the musician sings the praise of Bacchus, we are back into a frenzied double beat--"Sound the Trumpets; beat the Drums." When he sings the praise of Darius, we are back into a solemn, woeful dirge--"a Mournful Muse / Soft Pity to infuse." The oppositions of emotion and silence, pleasure and pain, battle and conquest all work their way into Dryden's poem. They are all "Happy Pairs."

We can sense the almost dizzying back and forth sway of the ode in its weighty double beat. That beat defines structure, with each stanza depicting a scene opposite in tone to the preceding and following stanza. It defines language, as we can see in such oxymoronic expressions as "present Deity" and "vanquish'd Victor." It defines repetitive motifs, such as the chorus at the end of each stanza, or the rhetorical twists of certain lines as "And sigh'd and look'd, sigh'd and look'd, / Sigh'd and look'd, and sigh'd again." The poem is filled with "Revolveing" motions that keep us whirling within a circle, constantly at odds with what the verse has forced us to feel only a moment before.

Few poems put their readers through such drastic oppositions of tone and response. We are presented, as Ehrenpreis has observed, with an apparently serious Pindaric ode, and yet its style is rollicking, a style that Mark Van Doren called "immortal ragtime."[37] But the rhythms are more violent than ragtime: we move from Jove's ravishment of Olympia to the soldier's bacchanal "Pleasure after Pain," which excite Alexander to fight "all his Battails o'er again." From there we are taken to the quiet solitude of Darius, left "With not a Friend to close his Eyes," a tone which moves Alexander to the soft pangs of love. But we are no sooner watching the victor vanquished by his lover than thunder and cries of revenge wake him, almost in nightmare fashion, to destroy the unburied ghosts of his battles. And thus the story seems to end. The power of music "Cou'd swell the Soul to rage, or kindle soft Desire."

Until "At last," Dryden tells us, "Divine *Cecilia* came." Here at the very end of the ode we seem to get a sense that the imagery of battle and passion and desire will be calmed by Cecilia's "heav'nly" music. She has, after all, "Enlarg'd the former narrow Bounds, / And added Length to solemn Sounds." But the most Dryden will give to the heavenly power of music is half the crown; indeed, the progress of his poem gives considerably less than that. What we end up with is not so much a sense of balance, but dual perspectives, divided visions--all defined by the power of music to move us in extremely different directions. We are still caught within the confines of the circle, and the final lines of the ode remind us of how easy it is, from this perspective, to mistake earth for heaven:

> Let old *Timotheus* yield the Prize,
> Or both divide the Crown;
> He rais'd a Mortal to the Skies;
> She drew an Angel down.

We are left somewhere between earth and heaven. Or perhaps it would be more correct to say that we are allowed a vision of earth in heaven as Timotheus raises a mortal to the skies, and heaven on earth as Cecilia draws the angel down. The power of the "double beat" has led us in two directions, where it is all too easy to mistake our final position.

To anyone familiar with the criticism written on *Alexander's Feast,* it must be obvious that what I am describing as Dryden's theme of doubles has in the past been described as a "problem" with the poem. One critic puts the matter this way: "The criticism as a whole suggests a poem that is (depending on your approach) brilliant, enigmatic, euphorious, disturbing, serious, meaningless, good-humored, disillusioned, celebratory and debunking; and as not all of these descriptions can apply without contradiction, even to so various a writer as Dryden, an attempt to reassess the poem is perhaps justified."[38] But as the list of descriptions indicates, the real "problem" with the ode is that we are not sure exactly how it should be taken: as serious or good-humored, celebration or condemnation, moral or immoral.

I am convinced that such descriptions are not contradictory--not to Dryden, at least, who by this time in his life had grown quite accustomed to the interplay of dual forces in his works. That, after all, was his "double beat." It was the way he could so willingly "divide the Crown." It was the "feast" that Alexander enjoyed in the poem. And, as we will see, it was Dryden's feast, too.

CHAPTER 2

Dryden and Notions of Duality

In his epistle to Charleton, which we should again remember was one of his earliest poems, Dryden relied on a variety of dual structures revolving around the opposition of science and philosophy. These two subjects happen to be particularly relevant to a study of Dryden's dualities since several notions of duality, as I will attempt to show in this chapter, have a rich background in the scientific and philosophical thought of the seventeenth century. I feel it imperative to study this matter of intellectual context not only because the question of Dryden's "milieu" and its influence on him has been a highly debated issue, but also because I will be offering a different slant to some of our accepted opinions about the nature of his age. My method will be to work from the assumption that Dryden is indeed a writer possessed of a dualistic vision, and thus to examine his intellectual context from this perspective. For without an idea of what the notion of duality *could* mean to Dryden in the seventeenth century, it would be impossible to understand how it characterized his thought and permeated his art, which is finally my main critical endeavor.

I have postponed until now a discussion of the term "duality," in part because I wanted first to discuss the kinds of doublings we can find in Dryden and in some of his works, and also because my reliance on the term is specific to its meaning in the seventeenth-century context. The habit of treating discourse in terms of oppositions is, after all, a fundamental thought process in Western culture and has, through the centuries, taken on a variety of forms and assumed a variety of labels--the Platonic division of body and soul, the Cartesian dualism of mind and body, the Hegelian conflict of thesis and antithesis. Indeed there are so many versions of philosophical duality that the notion becomes almost meaningless until it is defined in terms of some specific intellectual and historical context.

What I want to examine in this chapter are several contexts for the version of duality which engaged Dryden. In doing so, I will be focusing attention on three models of dualistic thought--the essays of Montaigne and Bacon, the intellectual atmosphere provided by late seventeenth-century science, and the philosophical discourse of Hobbes. Here I think we can uncover some implicit and explicit notions of duality that reflect a preoccupation, especially popular during the Renaissance and

26

seventeenth century, to seek knowledge through the conflict of opposites.[1]

In using the term "duality," then, I will be referring both to an historically based method of discourse and inquiry, as well as to a specific tendency of Dryden which shaped the structure, style, and meaning of his literary works. These two references of "duality" will obviously not always be the same--Hobbes's dualistic structures, for instance, are not Dryden's, and Dryden's are not Bacon's. Nonetheless, I am convinced that several important figures whom we have traditionally associated with Dryden shared a very similar kind of dualistic vision, one that was characterized by a markedly dualistic thought process. How Dryden relied on this process and what meaning he derived from the interplay of dualities is the subject of the final three chapters of this study, which examine the divisive forces at work in his best literary expressions. Now, however, I want to look at some notions of duality which help account for those divisive forces, and which help explain why an author who seems so integrated in his temperament can actually be quite divided in his statements and sympathies.

The Renaissance Background: Montaigne, Bacon

We can begin with the skeptical traditions associated with Montaigne and Bacon. I speak of traditions because, as recent criticism has shown, there were actually two kinds of skepticism that influenced Renaissance and seventeenth-century thought: classical philosophical skepticism, sometimes referred to as Pyrrhonism, which not only doubts the truth of particular subjects, but doubts the possibility of attaining ultimate knowledge and certitude; and a revisionist notion of skepticism, one which influenced the development of the scientific spirit, and which doubts the validity of immediate matters only as a means to some final knowledge.[2] What ties the two traditions together, then, is not their ends but their methodology. Much like the truth-error dichotomy in Dryden's epistle to Charleton, skepticism allows for the truth or falsity of any statement by considering its contrary. The methodology is fundamentally dualistic.

The philosophical skeptic Montaigne and the scientific philosopher Bacon both voiced the fundamental ideas that we now associate with the two traditions. They are also, of course, figures who have commonly been associated with Dryden's milieu and contexts. Bredvold, for instance, notes that Montaigne, and particularly those who followed in his tradition--Charron, LeVayer, Browne--"permeated English thought after the Restoration." Thomas Browne's informal essay style and skepticism, Bredvold continues, were especially "suggestive of Montaigne," and his witty paradoxes afforded some of the most popular reading during the Restoration, particularly within the court circle.[3] But it was Bacon who was the more immediately influential figure. He appears in the company of Charles and Viscount Brouncker on the frontispiece of Sprat's *History of the Royal Society*. And as we have seen, Dryden attributes to Bacon the present and future knowledge of the world in his epistle to Charleton. Phillip Harth suggests that the influence of Bacon at Trinity College, Cambridge--also the college of Dryden and Newton--shaped the "skeptical ideals" which he associates with both the Royal Society and Dryden's early writings.[4] Yet Bacon actually falls in the middle of a tradition, for as much as he influenced the spirit and method of scientific skepticism, so he inherited the basic notions of skepticism from his forerunners. His own intellectual milieu brought him into contact with the most important skeptical thought of the sixteenth century.[5] Indeed the connection between Montaigne and Bacon has long been recognized. Both shared the informal essay style, and there has been argument that "a greater concreteness of style" in Bacon's later essays is attributable to the influence of Montaigne.[6] It should not be surprising that certain elements of style were shared by the two outstanding essayists of the Renaissance, both of whom also shared the spirit, if not the exact philosophy, of skepticism. But the distinct element of style, actually a pattern of thought, which both essayists shared was their dualistic method of expression and analysis.

This method involves not only the opposition of contraries, of the kind we have seen in Dryden's epistle to Charleton, but also a reluctance to merge these differences into a synthesis. The reluctance bears a striking resemblance to the hesitation with which scientists approached hypotheses and conclusions, a hesitation we find in several treatises on the Royal Society, and particularly in the attitude of its outstanding member, Newton. The dialectic of Montaigne and Bacon, in this sense, might be seen as an example of the examining mind which constantly weighs the merits and demerits of dual sides of issues. More specifically, it is a model for the kind of dualistic vision that I find characteristic of Dryden and the age for which he spoke.

In his essay "Of the Art of conferring," Montaigne writes: "The world is but a Schoole of inquisition. The matter is not who shall put in, but who shall runne the fairest courses."[7] His essays are such an attempt. They constantly explore issues, but rarely derive conclusions. Indeed, any apparent conclusion is neither meaningful nor interesting, for as anyone who even skims the essays can readily see, their liveliness derives from the richness of argument and variety of examples. Yet Montaigne's thought was not random. He insisted that it be systematized, claiming "I shall quietly contest a whole day, if the conduct of the controversie be followed with order and decorum" (III.163). This sense of order which characterized Montaigne's discourse was its dualistic structure. One critic, for instance, sees Montaigne's "artistic attitude" as delighting "in paradox and ambiguity," and suggests that "his admiration for Socrates the debater"--who often refused to conclude his own arguments--accounts for Montaigne's playful argumentative style and his distrust of reason.[8]

We can find dual structures in various levels of Montaigne's essays. For instance, he will rarely address himself to one subject. The titles of the essays often rely on doublings which enhance their paradoxical meaning: "By divers meanes men come unto a like end," "The profit of one man is the dammage of another," "How we weepe and laugh at one self-same thing," "Of bad meanes emploied to a good end." Even when Montaigne does seem to focus on one topic, his mind automatically divides the issue into dual components:

> Now death, which some of all horrible things call the most horrible, who knows not, how others call it, the only haven of this lives-torments?
>
> (I.273-74)

> Moreover, this ought to comfort us, that naturally, if paine be violent, it is also short; if long, it is easie....
>
> (I.281)

> The Merchant thrives not but by the licentiousnesse of youth; the Husbandman by dearth of corne; the Architect but by the ruine of houses; the Lawyer by suits and controversies betweene men: Honour it selfe, and practice of religious Ministers, is drawne from our death and vices.
>
> (I.103)

> I give my soule one visage, and sometimes another, according unto the posture or side I lay her in. If I speake diversly of my selfe, it is because I looke diversly upon my selfe. All contrarieties are found in her, according to some turne or removing; and in some fashion or other. Shame-fast, bashfull, insolent, chaste, luxurious, peevish, pratling, silent, fond, doting, labourious, nice, delicate, ingenious, slow, dull, froward, humorous, debonaire, wise, ignorant, false-in-words, true-speaking, both liberall, covetous, and prodigall.... *Distinguo* is the most universall part of my logike.
>
> (II.10)

In such statements we not only see Montaigne dividing issues, but adopting a style fundamentally dualistic in its structure. Sentences and clauses typically oppose elements of discourse. Moreover, these smaller dual structures in turn govern the larger structures of discourse. Montaigne is constantly flipping his discussion over with phrases of the kind we constantly encounter, for instance, in his essay "Of the uncertainte of our judgement": "But why may not a man also hold the contrarie?" "And might also encline to the other side," "who might not also have said, that contrariwise..." (I.324-28). So fundamental were such double structures to his thought that on one occasion he wrote:

> This supple variation, and easie yeelding contradiction, which is seene in us, hath made some to imagine, that wee had two soules, and others, two faculties; whereof every one as best she pleaseth, accompanieth and doth agitate us; the one towards good, the other towards evill.
>
> (II.9-10)

Yet Montaigne would not even believe in this simple bifurcation of essence, insisting that what seems to be a general division of essence (two souls, two faculties) is in fact composed of a series of "contrarieties." We will see Hobbes approaching his philosophy in much the same way.

It is easy to understand how such a divided vision led Montaigne to skepticism. Yet his apparent belief that final knowledge is unattainable did not prevent him from sustaining his inquiry. It was as if once the process of inquiry was in motion, it simply could not be stopped. Montaigne said that he was willing to argue and discuss all day; in fact, he did just that for a lifetime. This constant effort to sustain the inquiry, even with full knowledge that no conclusions could be reached, is what marks him as a forerunner of the scientific spirit of inquiry. In distinguishing himself from philosophers, for instance, he distances himself from their logical and rational methodology, insisting that passion rather than reason inspires the philosopher:

> It is a meere divine inspiration, that sacred truth hath inspired in a Philosophicall spirit, which against his proposition exacteth from him; that the quiet state of our soule, the best-settled estate, yea the healthfullest that Philosophy can acquire unto it, is not the best estate. Our vigilancie is more drouzie, then sleepe it selfe: Our wisedome lesse wise, then folly; our dreames of more worth then our discourses.
>
> (II.288-89)

Not surprisingly, of the three men Montaigne considered most outstanding--Homer, Alexander the Great, and Epaminondas--none was a philosopher. Two were men of action. Alexander, of course, was the subject of one of Dryden's finest poems. And as for Homer, Montaigne writes that his words "are the onely words that have movement and action; they are the onely substantiall Wordes" (II.497-98).

"Action" is in fact exactly the right word to describe the lively inquiry of Montaigne. In a famous passage from his *Apology for Raymond Sebond,* he writes:

> In few, there is no constant existence, neither of our being, nor of the objects. And we, and our judgement, and all mortall things else do uncessantly rowle, turne, and passe away. Thus can nothing be certainely established, nor of the one, nor of the other; both the judgeing and the judged being in continuall alteration and motion.
>
> (II.329)

Such a statement might well define the limits of skepticism, but we will also see Bacon and Hobbes rely on the idea of motion and its dual forces. In fact, "continuall alteration and motion" is a principle that might well explain the method and inquiry of the new science. It is likely for this reason that we find Francis Bacon, the formative spokesman for the new science, engaged in a ceaseless discourse involving oppositions and dualities remarkably similar to Montaigne's.

In his own essays, Bacon typically addresses two sides of an issue. Margaret Wiley finds him constantly preoccupied with "paradox and dualisms," and Stanley Fish's study of "The Experience of Bacon's *Essays*" has done much to modify our traditional assumptions about Bacon's exactness and objectivity, calling attention instead to his commitment to the process of discovery and inquiry.[9] One of Bacon's favorite phrases, "On the other side," involves a method which, like Montaigne's, flips over issues to consider not only alternate but opposed arguments. Bacon's opening essay "Of Truth," for instance, is actually an essay on both the true and the false, truth and lies. Not surprisingly, Bacon quotes Montaigne, who supplies additional bifurcated commentary on falsehood: "Saith he, *If it be well weighed, to say that a man lieth, is as much as to say as, that he is brave towards God and a coward towards men.* For a lie faces God, and shrinks from man."[10] Not only is Bacon, here through Montaigne, "weighing" two notions of deceit, but he is also relying on two opposed movements--toward and away--for his vehicle of expression. Such double structures and double subjects can be found throughout the essays. Even in his own comments on the necessity to divide any dispatch, Bacon explains himself by considering the extreme opposite of each issue:

> Above all things, order, and distribution, and singling out of parts, is the life of dispatch; so as the distribution be not too subtle: for he that doth not divide will never enter well into business; and he that divideth too much will never come out of it clearly.
>
> (p. 163)

31

This division of argument is Bacon's fundamental approach to any kind of analysis.[11] And though he will often divide issues into several parts, he most often relies on double structures, especially for the most basic breakdown of issues. In his essay "Of Vicissitude of Things," he comments on the belief that "two things," fixed stars and diurnal motion, are constant in the universe, and that the "great winding-sheets, that bury all things in oblivion, are two; deluges and earthquakes" (p. 274). The very structure of his discourse "Of the Colours of Good and Evil" revolves around a dual consideration of each issue:

> ... nothing can be of greater use and defence to the mind, than the *discovering* and *reprehension* of these colours, showing in what cases they *hold*, and in what they *deceive*....
>
> (XIII. 269-70, italics mine)

The natural product of such a divided methodology is, of course, a style characterized by dual structures and balanced elements. Bacon will always explain how "some" do this and "others" do that, or how too much of one thing means too little of another. Advice is especially couched in these kinds of terms: "To use too many circumstances ere one come to the matter, is wearisome; to use none at all, is blunt" (p. 194).

Like Montaigne's style, Bacon's is calculating, where issues are constantly defined by what they are not, and where any sort of conclusion--as in Bacon's discourse on truth and lies--remains to be found somewhere between or even outside the discussion of opposites. Stanley Fish, for instance, finds in the essays continual qualification and amendment of original statements. It is Bacon's method to examine and reexamine, to reconsider and even retract. Describing "Of Marriage and Single Life," Fish observes one particular statement that contains "two discursive structures in a single space, and to the extent they pull against each other or point in different directions, the reader's experience of them is strenuous and, what is more important, inconclusive." The effect that Fish goes on to describe is remarkably similar to what we will find in Dryden, who was just as engaged in the "experience" of literature so characteristic of the seventeenth century. Referring to the "different directions" of Bacon's argument, Fish observes: "Not that one cancels out the other; rather, neither finally carries the day, with the result that the reader remains suspended between the conclusions each of them is separately urging, and ends by asking a question instead of assenting to an argument."[12] Few of Bacon's essays offer any sense of closure. Finalities and conclusions--though ultimately sought--were not a part of his thought process.

Also like Montaigne, Bacon was consumed with the process of his discourse. Though on several occasions he warns that idle argument can lead nowhere (he in fact specifically refers to the Pyrrhonists by saying "there be that delight in giddiness, and count it a bondage to fix a belief") (p. 6), he clearly could not escape the "delight" of his own argument, his own engagement in inquiry. His essay "Of Discourse," which bears some resemblance to Montaigne's on the art of discussion, indicates that he had a fondness for the process of argumentation quite like Montaigne's:

> The honourablest part of talk is to give the occasion; and again to moderate and pass to somewhat else; for then a man leads the dance. It is good, in discourse and speech of conversation, to vary and intermingle speech of the present occasion with arguments, tales with reasons, asking of questions with telling of opinions, and jest with earnest: for it is a dull thing to tire, and, as we say now, to jade, any thing too far.
>
> (p. 192)

Bacon never tired. And it was surely his commitment to inquiry about the "things" of the world that supplied him with a dialectic so appealing to the new science. He even cautions--again employing an antithetical form of statement--that we should not be alarmed by the multitude of particulars, but instead be hopeful on that very account ("Interim particularium multitudinem nemo reformidet, quin potius hoc ipsum ad spem revocet") (p. 318). The caution appropriately comes from his *Novum Organum,* a work which explains and incorporates the "method" of science. It also seems appropriate that this inquiry into the multifaceted "Nature of Things" was necessarily neither philosophical nor logical. Just as Montaigne had shunned the consistency and uniformity of philosophical systems, so Bacon, from the outset, distinguished between two forms of inquiry--yet another division that he relied on. There should be, he argued, two sources and distributions of knowledge ("duae doctrinarum emanationes, ac duae dispensationes"): one would be philosophical in its cultivation of the sciences ("sit denique alia scientias colendi"), the other would be scientific discovery itself ("alia inveniendi ratio") (p. 237). What immediately follows this division of philosophy and science is Bacon's description of the scientific spirit, one of constant searching and seeming endless inquiry. He invites those who are willing to use present knowledge as a vehicle for penetrating still further into the nature of things ("sed ad ulteriora penetrare") to join with the sons of science. Their aim will not be to present elegant opinions ("non belle et probabiliter opinari") but to know things to a certainty and demonstration ("sed certo et ostensive scire") (p. 237).

This mandate defined the spirit of the Royal Society. It was a mandate characterized by two major tendencies--the predilection to

33

examine phenomena in terms of dual and often contrary elements, and the propensity to engage in ongoing investigation, to penetrate still further and to know things to a certainty. I spoke earlier of how the concept of motion engaged the skeptic Montaigne. But motion was as well a part of the truth-seeking endeavor of Bacon. Wiley suggests that "what distinguishes the many dualisms discussed by Bacon is that they are always dualisms on the move," and appropriately quotes this statement of his: " 'Rational life, then, does not reflect static entities. Rational life involves movement, and its faculties and powers involve movement.' "[13] In Bacon's scientific system the best conclusions are by definition not conclusions at all, but grounds for further inquiry. Dryden's censure, in his epistle to Charleton, of the reign of only "one truth" reflects an outlook that Bacon and Montaigne--perhaps for different reasons--would have easily embraced; his subject division and stylistic oppositions in the epistle reflect a method that was inherent in the discourse of both essayists.

Seventeenth-Century Science: Newton

Thomas Sprat, in his *History of the Royal Society*, explained that it was the study of Nature, of "things," which distanced scientists from human affairs and made it possible for them to entertain divergent opinions: *"that* gives us room to differ, without animosity; and permits us, to raise contrary imaginations upon it, without any danger of a civil war."[14] The statement is by no means Sprat's only reference to the divisions and oppositions of scientific argument. Indeed the raising of "contrary imaginations" was a principle of inquiry for the Royal Society. Rejecting both dogmatism (one truth) and skepticism (no truth), the members of the Royal Society were willing to entertain as much diversity and contradiction as necessary. Of course theirs was not a relativist position. Truth was sought, but the means took precedence over the end. Bacon's own reservations about the formation of conclusions can be seen again and again in the opinions of these scientists.[15] Sprat summarizes the philosophical predicament in this way:

> ... this *doubtfulness* of thoughts, this *fluctuation*, this *slowness* of concluding, which is so useful in this case, is so natural to a multitude of Counsellors.... here, he that can make a *solid objection*, or ask a *seasonable question*, will do more good, than he, who shall boldly fix on a hundred *ill-grounded resolutions*.[16]

It was the very method of science, in other words, to debate and analyze dual sides of issues, and to view truth as the product of contention, not the end product of consistent argument. I want to focus on one of the

34

foremost examples of this dualistic investigative process inherent in the scientific method--the development of light theory in the late seventeenth century. But in order to do so, let me first shift focus to a twentieth-century scientific notion--that of "complementarity" in modern physics--which explains much of our present scientific theory and which, interestingly, derives from the physics of a late seventeenth-century scientist, Isaac Newton.

Complementarity in modern physics uses as its model two apparently contradictory theories about the nature of light--light as the movement of waves (wave theory) and light as the movement of particles (corpuscular theory). Since both theories are valid, and since both are needed for the explanation of other phenomena, they are said to coexist, to be complementary. Until the twentieth century, however, science did not embrace both concepts, and instead constantly vacillated between arguing for the correctness of one or the other. The argument actually predates Newton, but becomes particularly important when he made it an issue in his *Opticks*, a work which he completed during the final years of the Restoration. Yet what is particularly interesting about Newton's investigations into light theory is that, though he himself had no formal notion of scientific complementarity, the very nature of his inquiry was founded on dual contending arguments and hesitant open-ended conclusions.

Newton was writing on light theory as early as 1672, the year in which he presented a paper to the Royal Society on the relationship between light and color. During the ensuing years, at least until the publication of the *Opticks* in 1704, he was preoccupied with the nature of light, especially the wave versus corpuscular theories. He himself engaged in several debates on the question, notably with Christiaan Huygens. The controversies were long and involved, and Newton's ideas were clearly unsettled. Still, he finally did embrace the corpuscular theory in the *Opticks*, a theory which he relied on as a premise in order to explain the properties of light "by Reason and Experiments."[17] And yet, as several commentators have noted, Newton was reluctant to insist about the correctness of the corpuscular theory,[18] a reluctance apparent throughout the *Opticks*. Bernard Cohen explains: "Not only had Newton erred in his choice of the corpuscular theory, but also he apparently had found no insuperable difficulty in simultaneously embracing features of two opposing theories."[19] The dual nature of light theory, in other words, was not only a highly-debated issue in the late seventeenth century, but an issue actually composed of opposing theories which Newton himself neither could resolve, nor apparently wanted to resolve.

One of the reasons I stress this relationship between the notion of "complementarity" in modern physics and the dual seventeenth-century theories about the nature of light is that recently "complementarity" has been a term adopted by literary critics to explain Shakespeare's characteristic pattern of opposing his subjects. According to this literary view, Shakespeare's vision does not derive from "recurrent themes," but is instead a dual vision revolving around opposed themes. Yet as Norman Rabkin, one of the first critics to use "complementarity" in a literary sense, explains, the concept need not be restricted either to the twentieth century or to Shakespeare. He describes how Bohr and Oppenheimer, for instance, have applied the notion to "the ceaseless debate between theories of free will and determinism," and suggests that this dualistic outlook can be found in such diverse writers as Homer, Virgil, Dante, Chaucer, Cervantes, Goethe, Stendhal, Tolstoy, and Freud. We might even argue, according to Rabkin, that "the most poignant awareness of the complementary nature of human experience" is fundamentally "the stuff of art."[20]

It is easy to understand, however, why no author from the Restoration or eighteenth century appears on this list. If the notion of duality has been popularized in Shakespeare, it has been--with a few notable exceptions--curiously ignored in the writers of the age which immediately followed his. The omission is curious not only because the notion of complementarity has its roots in Newtonian physics which generated some of the formative theories about the nature of light, but also because dualistic and contrary structures were deeply embedded in the methodology of the most notable scientists and philosophers of the sixteenth and seventeenth centuries. In many ways, the "Breaking of the Circle"--which Nicolson attributes to the effects of the new science--was actually a splitting or division of the circle into two halves. There always seemed to be two different, sometimes contradictory, ways of viewing phenomena. And scientists were far more inclined to engage in this ongoing dialectic, consumed with the play of oppositions rather than the need to settle on conclusions and resolutions. Even Swift's satiric comment on the scientists of Laputa, "They are very bad Reasoners, and vehemently given to Opposition," is a quite accurate description of the movement away from reason and logic in scientific investigation.[21] The inquiry of science was open-ended, and we can look again to Newton for an excellent case in point.

The endings of Newton's two great works, the *Opticks* and the *Principia*, are not conclusions at all, but cautious endnotes on the danger of confirming conclusions which are neither supported by experimentation nor as yet fully examined. In the third edition of the *Opticks*, for instance, Newton added to the text what he called some "questions." One can easily sense in them the caution with which he framed his observations:

> All bodies *seem* to be composed of hard Particles.... Even the Rays of Light *seem* to be hard Bodies.... At least, this *seems* to be as evident as the universal Impenetrability of Matter. For all Bodies, *as far as Experience reaches*, are either hard, or may be harden'd; and we have no other Evidence of universal Impenetrability, besides a large Experience without an experimental Exception.
>
> (p. 389, italics mine)

The statement is not a reflection of Newton's personal hesitation as a scientist, but rather an axiomatic principle of scientific methodology. In explaining this methodology, Newton distinguished between observed phenomena (experiments, observations, temporary conclusions drawn from induction) and their causes ("occult Qualities, supposed to result from specifick Forms of Things") (pp. 401-4). Not only did he not engage in moving, as he said, "from Effects to their Causes," but believed that "Such occult Qualities put a stop to the improvement of natural Philosophy, and therefore of late Years have been rejected" (p. 401). All conclusions from induction must be open ended, not final:

> For Hypotheses are not to be regarded in experimental Philosophy. And although the arguing from Experiments and Observations by Induction be no Demonstration of general Conclusions; yet it is the best way of arguing which the Nature of Things admits of.... And if no Exception occur from Phenomena, the Conclusion may be pronounced generally. But if at any time afterwards any Exception shall occur from Experiments, it may then begin to be pronounced with such Exceptions as occur.
>
> (p. 404)

The spirit of this scientific method--the reluctance to form general conclusions, the refusal to proceed from effects to causes--is nowhere more apparent than in the famous *Scholium Generale* which Newton attached to the *Principia*. This brief afterword exists in several versions, and in each revision we can sense Newton's stronger disdain for the formation of hypotheses: "I do not frame hypotheses," he insists *("hypotheses non fingo")*.[22] Indeed one of the last statements that Newton wrote about his *Principia* is contained in a letter to Roger Cotes, editor of the second edition. Having already corresponded with Cotes several times about the wording of the *Scholium*, Newton finally writes:

> Experimental Philosophy proceeds only upon Phenomena & deduces general Propositions from them only by

Induction.... And he that in experimental Philosophy would except against any of these must draw his objection from some experiment or phaenomenon & not from a mear Hypothesis, if the Induction be of any force.[23]

The history of the development of light theory, and particularly Newton's contribution to that theory, fulfills his own belief in the process of constant examination and reexamination of phenomena. The corpuscular theory, for instance, which Newton used as a premise in his *Opticks*, was almost totally rejected in the nineteenth century, only to be revived and proved by Einstein in the twentieth century--thus giving rise to the very notion of complementarity which allows for the two opposing theories of light to coexist. It is a strange turn of science that a famous scientific dualism of the seventeenth century--concerning light theory-- has been confirmed as a valid dualism by twentieth-century science and its notions of complementarity. Complementarity was, therefore, first a notion in tune with the raising of "contrary imaginations," a fundamental process of seventeenth-century science. But it is also a notion which reflects our conviction that truths in literature are no more simplistic and no less complicated than truths in science.

Seventeenth-Century Philosophy: Hobbes

It seems appropriate to end a discussion of seventeenth-century dualistic preoccupations with Thomas Hobbes, a figure whose influence on Dryden and whose relationship with the Royal Society have been examined from a variety of perspectives. And yet my inclusion of Hobbes-- though it does derive in part from these relationships--is based on his own very definite system of dualities. In Hobbes, I think, we can see an extremely precise expression of dualistic thought, and also the philosophical culmination of many of the dualistic notions found in Montaigne, Bacon, and the new science.

We can begin with the illustrated title page of *Leviathan*.[24] The page is divided into two halves, top and bottom. In the top section we see the figure of the king who holds a sword in one hand, a sceptre in the other. The king himself contains a multitude of persons--symbolic of Hobbes's contract between the people and their monarch. The bottom of the page is divided into two halves, left and right, each side composed of five symbols. In one column, directly under the king's sword, we find pictures associated with battle: fortress, weapons, a depiction of two armies in conflict. In the other column, we find pictures associated with stability and order: church, insignia of unity, a depiction of a court of justice. Obviously this title page suggests a wealth of dualities, all of which revolve around several major oppositions: the opposition of one and many, of civil and ecclesiastical, of conflict and stability.

38

In one sense, these are the political oppositions which shape the political philosophy of Hobbes: through the great leviathan figure of the commonwealth, through the process of contract, dualities and differences are balanced. But in another sense, the pictoral oppositions of the title page are indicative of the profound dualistic nature of Hobbes's very thought. His philosophical assumptions, for instance, are all based on two opposed movements: desire and aversion. Once this duality is postulated, every other aspect of the nature "Of Man"--a philosophical discourse which is the foundation of Hobbes's social and political thought--can be explained. This basic duality literally generates a host of others, forming a process of generation which moves from explaining the simplest sensations to the most complex human passions.

The interdependence and generation of dualities begins with Hobbes's discussion of "Voluntary Motions; Commonly Called The Passions." In this passage from the opening of Chapter VI of *Leviathan*, we can watch Hobbes progress from a consideration of two kinds of motion to the two basic directions of motion:

> There be in animals, two sorts of *motions* peculiar to them: one called *vital* ... the other is *animal motion,* otherwise called *voluntary motion....* These small beginnings of motion, within the body of man, before they appear in walking, speaking, striking, and other visible actions, are commonly called ENDEAVOUR.
> This endeavour, when it is toward something which causes it, is called APPETITE, or DESIRE.... And when the endeavour is fromward something, it is generally called AVERSION. These words, *appetite* and *aversion,* we have from the Latins; and they both of them signify the motions, one of approaching, the other of retiring.[25]

On the basis of these two opposite motions Hobbes is able to account for the variety of human passions: love and hate, for instance, directly derive from appetite and aversion: "That which men desire, they are also said to LOVE: and to HATE those things for which they have aversion" (p. 32). The same situation applies to good and evil: "But whatsoever is the object of any man's appetite or desire, that is it which he for his part calleth *good:* and the object of his hate and aversion, *evil"* (p. 32). The listing of dual passions is extended, with each passion defined both by its opposite and its relationship to those which precede it: Pulchrum-Turpe, Delightful-Unpleasant, Profitable-Unprofitable, Pleasures of Sense-Pleasures of Mind, Ambition-Pusillanimity, Liberality-Miserableness, Sudden Glory-Sudden Dejection, Laughter-Weeping. The listing of contraries recalls Montaigne and his constant pairing and opposition of issues, particularly his summation of the passions which divide his own personality.

Also reminiscent of Montaigne, as well as of Bacon, is Hobbes's consideration of "Discourse." Though the ideas Hobbes expresses are distinctly his own, they are also a rehashing of assumptions that we have previously associated with the traditions of skepticism and scientific inquiry.

> No discourse whatsoever, can end in absolute knowledge of fact, past, or to come. For, as for the knowledge of fact, it is originally, sense; and ever after, memory. And for the knowledge of consequence, which I have said before is called science, it is not absolute, but conditional.
>
> (p. 40)

In passages such as these we can see the relationship between conflicting and yet remarkably interdependent theories. But more importantly, we can see the workings of the same kind of thought process, one which naturally lends itself to dual methodologies and unresolved, temporary conclusions. Montaigne's belief that all things are "in continual change and motion," Bacon's discontent with "present discoveries" and his desire "to penetrate still further," and Hobbes's insistence that all knowledge and discourse are "conditional," each bears a definite resemblance to the other, giving a different perspective to basically the same issue. We will find Dryden just as susceptible to the flux of continuing and conditional knowledge, just as anxious to explore possibilities that do not lead to final conclusions.

This pattern of thought, which I believe came very naturally to all these writers, was particularly characteristic of Hobbes's own writing style. As with both Montaigne and Bacon, Hobbes automatically expressed himself in terms of oppositions, even when his argument did not warrant doing so. In his dedicatory letter to Francis Godolphin, prefixed to *Leviathan,* notice how Hobbes will vacillate between dual sides of issues within his very sentence structure:

> I know not how the world will receive it, nor how it may reflect on those that shall seem to favour it. For in a way beset with those that contend, on one side for too great liberty, and on the other side for too much authority, 'tis hard to pass between the points of both unwounded. But yet, methinks, the endeavour to advance the civil power, should not be by the civil power condemned....

We will also see Dryden relying on such stylistic vacillation, not merely the result of rhetorical balance or closed couplet rhetoric, but the product of a thought pattern severely divided in its methods of analysis and expression, and notably inconclusive in its final deliberations.

Hobbes's own finalities were imposed agreements, which is to say

40

they were balanced dualities, not reconciled oppositions. F.S. McNeilly, for instance, has discussed several dual and often "incompatible" accounts of phenomena in Hobbes, attributing this tendency in him to his commitment to mathematics as a model for knowledge. For in mathematics, McNeilly explains, "There seems to be no reason for supposing that there may not be many possible different sets of consistent postulates...."[26] Here again we find a notion very akin to that of complementarity in physics. Hobbes relied on such a complementary model for his idea of contract, which he defines as nothing more than the "mutual transferring of right" (p. 87). The very existence of contract is dependent on two opposed laws of nature, each of which defines the other--"to seek peace," and "to defend ourselves." Hobbes explains: "For as long as every man holdeth this right, of doing any thing he liketh; so long are all men in the condition of war" (p. 85). Hobbes's contract, then, allows for the coexistence of opposites--peace and battle--oppositions which recall the two basic motions of appetite and aversion, and which ultimately gloss the pictoral oppositions which appear on the title page of *Leviathan*. Drawing again on his mathematical model, Hobbes finally explains the nature of contract in terms of a "sum":

> And though this may seem too subtle a deduction of the laws of nature, to be taken notice of by all men; whereof the most part are too busy in getting food, and the rest too negligent to understand; yet to leave all men inexcusable, they have been contracted into one easy sum, intelligible even to the meanest capacity; and that is, *Do not that to another, which thou wouldest not have done to thyself*....
> (p. 103)

If Hobbes brings his discourse to a conclusion, it is clearly a conclusion composed of dualities, or as he himself might say, not absolute but conditional. It not only allows for the coexistence of opposites; it depends on them. Hobbes presents us with a dialectic in which oppositions are resolved only through the interplay of the very oppositions themselves.

The traditional skepticism of Montaigne, the scientific skepticism of Bacon, the scientific method of Newton, the dualistic philosophy of Hobbes--in these outlooks we can find some of the major sources and manifestations of dualistic thought in the seventeenth century. At times in them we can sense the workings of an intentionally unresolved dialectic; at other times we can sense an almost unconscious pattern of thought which predisposes itself to doubling and division. But whether conscious or unconscious, these notions of duality shaped some of the most important discourse of the age. I have tried to sketch the outlines of

41

this dualistic thought process and to suggest some reasons for its presence. And I have intentionally chosen for models figures who have, in some fashion or another, been traditionally associated with Dryden. Since my arguments do not insist on their direct influence on Dryden (those arguments have a context all their own),[27] I am content to have identified a pattern of thought that moves beyond ideological and philosophical differences, and can cross as well over the lines that separate prose discourse and literary expression. As I have said before, Dryden's dualities may not necessarily reflect the substance of those we find in Bacon or Hobbes, but while watching his dualities unfold, we can easily see similarities in kind and type. In the remaining chapters, I will be examining the forms these dualities assume in Dryden--dramatic interplay, political vicissitude, and religious indecision.

CHAPTER 3

Duality as Structure: The Divided Worlds of *All For Love*

"Fate comes too fast upon my wit,
Hunts me too hard, and meets me at each double."

Johnson, who was not always pleased with Dryden's "wild and daring sallies," once offered as an example of the poet's "warmth of fancy and haste of composition" this line from *The Indian Emperor:*

I follow fate, which does too fast pursue.

Here is Johnson's explanation of the "blunder":

> That no man could at once follow and be followed was, it may be thought, too plain to be long disputed; and the truth is, that DRYDEN was apparently betrayed into the blunder by the double meaning of the word FATE, to which in the former part of the verse he had annexed the idea of FORTUNE, and in the latter that of DEATH; so that the sense only was, *though pursued by* DEATH, *I will not resign myself to despair, but will follow* FORTUNE, *and do not suffer what is appointed.* This, however, was not completely expressed, and DRYDEN, being determined not to give way to his critics, never confessed that he had been surprised by an ambiguity; but finding luckily in *Virgil* an account of a man moving in a circle, with this expression, *Et se sequiturque fugitque,* 'Here,' says he, 'is the passage in imitation of which I wrote the line that my critics were pleased to condemn as nonsense; not but I may sometimes write nonsense, though they have not the fortune to find it.'[1]

Johnson's objections are obvious: Dryden not only committed an error, but was too stubborn to admit it. Yet if Johnson blames Dryden both for the mistake and for feigning an excuse, he nonetheless offers a generous explanation for the poet's shortcomings:

> Every one sees the folly of such mean doublings to escape the pursuit of criticism; nor is there a single reader of this poet, who would not have paid him greater veneration, had

he shewn consciousness enough of his own superiority to set such cavils at defiance, and owned that he sometimes slipped into errors by the tumult of his imagination, and the multitude of his ideas.

Three critical points are at issue here. First, Johnson accuses Dryden of being misled "by the double meaning of the word FATE." Second, he censures him for his stubborness, for "being determined not to give way to his critics," and "luckily" finding in Virgil a source for his paradoxical line. Then, finally, in almost forgiving fashion, Johnson excuses both the word error and "mean doubling" with Virgil, claiming that Dryden was inclined to commit such blunders because, after all, his imagination was in a state of tumult, his ideas were multitudinous. This strange turn of criticism at the end of Johnson's commentary may seem a bit out of tune with the severity of his accusations, but Johnson had written such things about Dryden before, and he recognized--perhaps more than most--the dexterous cast of Dryden's mind. If the critic could not accept the poet's doublings, he could at least uncover and accept their source in the poet himself.

Dryden wrote *The Indian Emperor* in 1665. In 1672, he defended the particular line which Johnson later described as nonsense by insisting that he took the line from Virgil.[2] It may seem unlikely that in 1677, when Dryden wrote about fate and doubling in *All For Love*, that he had in mind his troublesome line from *The Indian Emperor* -- but it is tempting to think so. For when Alexas voices much the same thought in the final act of *All For Love*, he is also caught in the middle of a vicious circle:

> Fate comes too fast upon my wit,
> Hunts me too hard, and meets me at each double.
>
> (255-56)

As with his line in *The Indian Emperor,* Dryden here too seems betrayed, as Johnson might say, by the double meaning of the word "fate." In one sense, Alexas's fate is his fortune--the fate which he pursues. He has just, at this point in the play, reconciled Antony to Cleopatra by making up a story about her suicide, and in doing so, has also managed to save himself from the wrath of Antony. "Good!" he congratulates himself, "The joy to find / She's yet alive completes the reconcilement. / I've saved myself and her" (252-54). To save himself--that is the "fate" Alexas pursues. But in another sense, Alexas's fate is his death--the fate which pursues him. Reconciling Antony and Cleopatra is not enough, for the Egyptian empire is crumbling, and Rome stands ready to conquer. Caught in this trap, Alexas can only continue his statement with "I've saved myself, and her. But, oh! The Romans!" The onslaught of Rome--that is the "fate" which pursues Alexas.

44

And that must also be what Alexas means when he says that fate "meets me at each double." Like an animal doubling back on his tracks, he tries to escape by moving in two directions. But his fate hunts him in two directions, trapping him within the double confines of his own trail. Nor is this by any means the only instance of doubling in the play. Antony and Cleopatra also find their "fate" urging them in opposite directions, ultimately meeting them "at each double." When Antony responds to the "fatal summons" of Cleopatra, he too is caught within a circle, deserts his own forces in battle, and can only exclaim: "I knew not that I fled, / But fled to follow you" (II.311-12). Cleopatra constantly finds herself standing on a pivot point. Her very first lines show her dilemma: "What shall I do, or whither shall I turn?" (II.1). It is a question that she will only be able to answer immediately before her death when, applying the aspics, she chooses the fate of Antony and demands: "O turn me to him, / And lay me on his breast!" (V.498-99). The fate of these lovers is at once their life and death, their passion and doom, their union and separation:

> Antony. Well, madam, we are met.
> Cleopatra: Is this a meeting?
>   Then we must part?
> Antony. We must.
> Cleopatra. Who says we must?
> Antony. Our own hard fates.
> Cleopatra. We make those fates ourselves.
> Antony. Yes, we have made 'em; we have loved each other
>   Into our mutual ruin.
>
> (II.241-45)

Dryden, despite what Johnson had to say on this matter, must surely have understood the double meaning of the word "fate." Indeed, he must have understood it in a far more complicated fashion than his own contemporary critics or Johnson ever suspected. It is this complicated notion of doubling and division, the way that Dryden seems always to split issues at the very moment he defines them, that is so characteristic of his cast of mind. It is also indicative of the kinds of dualisms we continually encounter in *All For Love*. Things are not whole, complete, unified. Instead, they are constantly under the pressure of opposing forces which threaten to split them apart. And that is true not only of the characters' fate, but of the world in which they live, the actions they take, the language they use.

Why I have chosen *All For Love* to begin my study of Dryden's dualities must be obvious. There has, after all, been so much controversy about the questionable "unity" of the play. Either directly or indirectly, commentators have continually addressed themselves to the drama's dualities which take on different forms in the hands of different critics. Johnson's censure, for instance, of the apparently crossed intentions and achievements of Dryden in *All For Love* is all too familiar to most scholars: the play, he tells us, "has one fault equal to many, though rather moral than critical, that by admitting the romantick omnipotence of Love, he has recommended as laudable and worthy of imitation that conduct which through all ages the good have censured as vicious, and the bad despised as foolish."[3] This "split" between intention and achievement has been at the core of the controversy surrounding the play.[4] For if we have not seen *All For Love* as manifesting a certain "fault" of Dryden, we have surely viewed the play as involving a series of conflicts which Dryden--depending on your point of view--either successfully reconciled or delibebrately left unsettléd. Eugene Waith, for instance, associates the theme of oppositions in the play with the myth of Hercules, Earl Miner treats the drama's contrary worlds as reflective of "conflicting motives" in Dryden himself, Derek Hughes offers a Hobbesian reading of the play and argues that it exposes the "conflict, instability, and unpredictability of nature," Frank Kearful studies the psychological tension in the drama, and Douglas Canfield explores the traditional opposition of "mutability and constancy" which the play embodies.[5]

But despite their emphasis on the various kinds of conflicts and oppositions which Dryden worked with in *All For Love,* critics seem to be in agreement that Dryden himself had some overriding single vision to offer, some way either to reconcile or explain the conflicts inherent in his play. Miner, for example, puts the matter this way: "there is but one man responding, attempting to divide his interests by exploring the limits of his forms and by searching for a 'perfect balance'...."[6] Even Hughes, who-- as he himself admits--postulates "a far greater complexity and subtlety in Dryden's handling and questioning of his characters' ideals than any previous criticism has done," nonetheless sees the "incompatible visions of reality" in the play as reflecting Dryden's own design which has affinities particularly with the ideas of Hobbes and Epicurus.[7] We might summarize the main assumptions of the critics in this way: though Dryden's drama is clearly about conflict, about two opposing world views and the tragedy which that opposition engenders, Dryden nonetheless controlled his subject and his vision of the story, and presented us with a cohesive, unified play.

I would suggest, however, that just the reverse is the case: the subject and vision of *All For Love* controlled Dryden. Johnson, I think, was very right in detecting not only the sympathy Dryden had for the world of the lovers, but the way Dryden seemed--almost in spite of himself--to

46

recommend and approve of that world. The play, in other words, is not only about the conflict of two world views, but about Dryden's own stake in that conflict--his inability to decide between the irreconcilable choices which the play itself presents. And we can sense Dryden's conflict--his submission to the dual forces in the drama--in his continual doublings and divisions which, instead of moving toward dramatic unity, ultimately solidify oppositions and divisions.

Of course Dryden inherited a story that was already structured around dualities: the opposing worlds of Egypt and Rome; the opposing characters of Antony and Caesar, Cleopatra and Octavia; the opposing demands of passion and duty. Especially in Shakespeare's *Antony and Cleopatra* he could find his models for dualistic structures.[8] But if Dryden's version of the story of Antony and Cleopatra is not more powerful than Shakespeare's in its expression of dualistic vision, it surely defines that dualistic outlook in a far more precise fashion. Dryden gave his drama two titles, *All For Love, Or The World Well Lost.* Just as we saw Dryden split the notion of fate by forcing his characters to confront their fate "at each double," so we can see him double and divide the play's very title. In one sense, its meaning pivots on the conjunction "or" (these lovers have nobly offered "All" for their love, and yet they have "Lost" the world). In another sense, it pivots on the double meaning of the word "well" (the world was indeed lost / the world was well worth the losing). We are given, in other words, no single notion of what the play is about; instead, it seems to be about the power of love *or* the loss of the world, about the righteousness of the lovers' defeat *or* the splendor of their personal victory. Here, I think, is Dryden's juxtaposition of theme, a juxtaposition that does not present us with two alternatives from which we should choose but, as Rabkin has said of Shakespeare's *Antony and Cleopatra*, dramatizes the "unresolvable dialectic between opposed values that claim us equally" and the "necessary tragedy of choice."[9]

If my remarks sound as though they might better be applied to Shakespeare's world of "mighty opposites" than to Dryden's apparent world of moral imperatives, we should remember that to a large extent Dryden's dramatic practice was founded on a variety of dual structurings. Ehrenpreis reminds us, for instance, that Dryden typically does not "prepare for the denouement of his plot by a dramatic chain," but instead relies on "a culmination of themes, images, and foreshadowings, by symmetries and reversals that amass the figurative language to be employed in the final scenes."[10] And we should also keep in mind Dryden's own fondness for dramatic paradox which, Alan Fisher claims, expresses for Dryden a sense of "dissatisfaction with what he knows is true."[11] That may very well be the crucial issue in *All For Love:* we cannot have things both ways.[12] But neither can we satisfactorily choose one alternative over the other. And so, we enter the world of paradox, of symmetry and reversal--the very Shakespearean world of mighty opposites.

I suggested earlier that Dryden's vision, if not more powerful than Shakespeare's in its expression of oppositions, was nonetheless more precise in its articulation of dualities. Much in the same way that Hobbes saw oppositions as engendering more oppositions,[13] so Dryden became consumed in the course of his play with the continual process of division. I want to examine this process, to trace its development and follow its directions. We can begin by looking at the way Dryden introduces dual structures in Act I--in the opening exchanges between Serapion and Alexas, Alexas and Ventidius, and finally Ventidius and Antony. We will see these dualities assume various structural forms: character oppositions, juxtaposed directional movements, circular images, language divisions. These are not only structures that define dualities, but they are the vehicles which Dryden uses to set up the final dual structure of his play.

Serapion is priest, interpreter of the gods--the ideal director of the play's action; Alexas is schemer, pander for Cleopatra and Antony--the real director of the play's action. The characters we first encounter, in other words, are drastically juxtaposed, and their initial exchange defines the two directions in which the action can move: upward, buoyed by the flood waters of the Nile to "th'utmost margin of the watermark" (8), or downward, floundering with sea creatures left in the muddy banks of the flood's retreat. In a vision, Serapion foresees Egypt's doom; in the real world, Alexas continues to scheme and plot.

Several commentators have discussed the oppositions which present themselves at the play's opening. Miner, for instance, calls them the "ambiguous expression of alternatives," with the Nile suggesting both creation and destruction.[14] And Fisher has described the opposition of Alexas and Serapion in terms of a "debate" between the two characters, arguing that the result is "a standoff; two ways of thinking and feeling about the world meet head on, and neither seems more solid than the other."[15] This all seems true enough for a description of what happens in the play. But I think the initial oppositions are even more revealing of Dryden's own opposed directional inclinations. Like both Serapion and Alexas, he will move the play in two opposite directions (toward the destruction of Egypt and the merger of the two lovers), and like the rise and fall of the Nile he will move the fates of characters in opposite directions (toward life, paradoxically associated with the loss of Egypt, and toward death, paradoxically assoicated with the victory of the lovers). I use the word "paradox" because life, after all, should rightly be associated with the fertility of Egypt and death with the military destructiveness of Rome. Instead, however, symmetry becomes reversal. And that reversal will dictate the crossed fates of the two characters who open the play: Alexas will be victim to the doom of the portents, while Serapion will survive to close the action of the drama.

We also discover, through their initial exchange, the larger structural divisions of the play's world. Rome and Egypt stand quietly juxtaposed: "war seems on either side to sleep" (57). Yet the balance will not hold. Appropriately, Serapion describes the grand reconciling image of potential balance--the image of power through union:

> While Antony stood firm, our Alexandria
> Rivaled proud Rome (dominion's other seat),
> And Fortune, striding like a vast Colossus,
> Could fix an equal foot of empire here.
>
> (67-70)

And, appropriately, Alexas offers an opposite scheme of balance--the image of power through division:

> Had I my wish, these tyrants of all nature
> Who lord it o'er mankind, should perish, perish,
> Each by the other's sword....
>
> (71-73)

In an ideal world, opposites balance. But in the real world, as Alexas goes on to remind us, we must choose in order to survive:

> but since our will
> Is lamely followed by our pow'r, we must
> Depend on one, with him to rise or fall.
>
> (73-75)

It is the inevitability of making a choice, of not being able to have things both ways, that defines the tension of the play's duelling forces. And not surprisingly, Alexas depicts this choice in terms of leading and following, also defining for the first time in the play the circular confines of action-- things concurrently pursuing and following each other. And so we encounter circular images, defining for us the power of both union and division. We can see these images, for instance, in the union of Antony and Cleopatra--in the circular embraces of Cleopatra which Alexas describes (she "winds herself about [Antony's] mighty ruins," 78), in the wreaths that Serapion calls for in celebration of Antony's birthday ("With laurels crowned; with laurels wreathe your posts," 146). But we also find them in the separation of the lovers (as when Alexas wishes Antony "divided from her arms / Far as the earth's deep center," 84-85, or when Ventidius describes Cleopatra leading Antony "in golden bands to gaudy slaughter," 171). Such circular structures--of winding movement, of wreaths, of "golden bands" and other jewels--provide Dryden with a dimension for his duelling forces. Their circumference describes the confines of the lovers, but also describes the circumference of the globe, wherein two half worlds wage war with each other.

The play opens, then, with the juxtaposition of Serapion and Alexas, priest and pander; it then moves to a confrontation between Alexas and Ventidius, both servants to their masters, yet each strikingly different in methods and aims. The final character opposition in the first act is of course the confrontation of Ventidius and Antony, a scene which Dryden said in his "Preface" he preferred "to anything which I have written in this kind" (p. 26). Even if we cannot trust Dryden's statement, we can be sure that he felt the culmination of oppositions in this scene, not only in the juxtaposition of these two similar yet different characters, but also within the very character of Antony himself, a character who ought to be, as Dryden tells us, a hero neither "of perfect virtue ... nor yet altogether wicked" (p. 12). Ventidius, we might say, is truly Antony's opposite. He is completely loyal to Rome, and yet will not desert his friend. Antony, on the other hand, wavers in his loyalty to both friend and country: "For, if a friend," he tells Ventidius, "thou hast beheld enough; / And, if a foe, too much" (260-61). Ventidius is sure of himself and his cause; Antony is confused. He can easily be swayed by the lures of Cleopatra or the urgings of Ventidius. He is inclined to move in two directions. That is his own division of character.

In this opening scene we also see the kinds of warring forces which will shape the action of the drama. The confrontation between Antony and Ventidius is quite typical of the kinds of confrontation that occur throughout the play: characters argue--battle with language--until one of them conquers. Then the scene reverses, characters again confront and argue, until another conquers. Within the dimensions of these arguments, language itself becomes divided. We encounter a variety of oxymoronic expressions (Ventidius accusing Cleopatra of making "perdition pleasing," 172, or describing Antony as "wondrous mournful," 209). There is also the opposition implied in the words "leave" and "love," an opposition we encounter on several occasions throughout the play (Antony ordering Ventidius, "Leave me," and Ventidius replying "Sir, I love you," 248-49, then later Antony insisting that he will give up Cleopatra: "And I will leave her; though, heav'n knows, I love / Beyond life, conquest, empire, all but honor; / But I will leave her," 422-24). Sometimes language is divided in its meaning, as when Antony accuses Ventidius of speaking "not half thou think'st," 284). Other times language must be doubled for the meaning to be sufficiently clear, as when Ventidius explains why his legions will not yet join with Antony:

> Ventidius. They said they would not fight for Cleopatra.
> Antony. What was't they said?
> Ventidius. They said they would not fight for Cleopatra.
>   (357-59)

This particular doubling of language works on several levels: it nicely complements the division of character (Antony/Ventidius), which in turn complements division of the army's loyalty (Antony/Cleopatra), which in turn complements division of the world (Egypt/Rome). The play will continue to present us with such divisions, until it finally solidifies a multiplicity of oppositions, leaving us with a vision rent apart by the force of contraries.

I have been trying to show that *All For Love* begins by setting forth a variety of dual structural motifs. We are introduced to a world grossly out of balance. In one sense, Antony tips the scales with his "double pomp of sadness":

> Why was I *raised* the meteor of the world,
> Hung in the skies, and blazing as I traveled,
> Till all my fires were spent, and then cast *downward*
> To be trod out by Caesar?
>   (206-9, italics mine)

In another sense, Cleopatra tips the scales, as Ventidius claims:

> See Europe, Afric, Asia, put in balance,
> And all weighed *down* by one light, worthless woman!
>   (371-72, italics mine)

We are also introduced to characters out of balance, some with each other, some with themselves. Thus the drama opens not with chaos, but polarities. Action is not random, but circular. Language is used not for straightforward statement, but argument and debate. These are Dryden's structural dualities in *All For Love*. By the end of the first act, he has set them all in motion.

I have said that Dryden was extremely precise in his definition of dual structures, and I might easily argue further that he not only formed them precisely, but exploited their inherent differences, sharpened their oppositions almost with a kind of vengeance. One of the most interesting examples is the confrontation of Cleopatra and Octavia, a confrontation Dryden defends in his "Preface" against accusations that he might offend "the greatness of their characters and the modesty of their sex" (p. 14). What is perhaps most revealing about Dryden's defense is that he justifies the confrontation on the basis of its realistic and powerful oppositions.

51

The very language of battle--of opposition--colors his explanation: "I judged it both natural and probable," he writes, "that Octavia, proud of her new-gained conquest, would search out Cleopatra to triumph over her, and that Cleopatra, thus attacked, was not of a spirit to shun the encounter." Interestingly, Dryden's depiction of these "two exasperated rivals" not only capitalizes on their opposition to each other, but on Dryden's own opposition to the "French poets" who, he tells us, would shun such confrontations or who, at best, would have their characters exchange "some cold civilities" rather than demonstrate "eagerness of repartee." Even more interesting is that Dryden, in the midst of his own battle with his critics, quotes "Honest Montaigne" in his defense. And it should not be surprising that he takes a passage from the essay "Of Presumption," one wherein Montaigne offers his own oppositions of ceremony and substance which Dryden in turn uses to justify his realistic (substantial) rather than polite (ceremonious) portrayal of the women (pp. 14-15). We might say, then, that a series of oppositions are at work in this scene involving Cleopatra and Octavia. There is, of course, their own confrontation in the play, then Dryden's confrontation with his critics, and finally--through Dryden's argument--Montaigne's confrontation with the critics. This superimposition of duelling forces, it seems to me, reveals a notably ingrained predilection for oppositions on Dryden's part, and a remarkably precise treatment of them in both the text of his play and the commentary in his preface.

Yet the actual confrontation of Cleopatra and Octavia is an example of only one kind of character opposition in the drama. It is straightforward and direct, involving none of the undercurrent of conflicting feelings that we saw, for instance, in the confrontation of Antony and Ventidius, or that we might find in the exchanges between Antony and Octavia or between Cleopatra and Dolabella. Still, the head-on confrontation of the two women is a fine example of clear-cut division and, more importantly, reminds us that the delight Dryden takes in establishing dualities has very little to do with the power of reconciliation.

The scene itself is pivotal since it falls in the middle of the play, near the end of Act III. It follows the union of Antony and Octavia and Dolabella--and yet precedes the more tangled confrontations of Dolabella and Cleopatra and Antony. And it involves a series of doubles and divisions. There are two women, united in their love for Antony. But all the rest is division: one is a "queen," the other a "Roman" (418-19); one has the "title of a wife," the other the "name of mistress" (460,465). Their actions are juxtaposed: Cleopatra forces Antony "To be a slave in Egypt," Octavia comes "To free him thence" (423-24). Their very relationship with Antony is split, as Cleopatra says, between the claims of legality and passion: "In my esteem, is he whom law calls yours, / But whom his love made mine" (434-35). Even their different powers to please Antony are neatly divided: Octavia accuses Cleopatra of an excess of charms which have "usurped my right" (436); Cleopatra's counterattack is that Octavia has not "half these charms" (440). It is this kind of intensity and bitterness of confrontation that shows how Dryden sharpens his oppositions with a vengeance.

Ventidius and Alexas are also diametrically opposed, both in substance (one acts out of loyalty to his friend, the other schemes to save himself) and in their dramatic functions (Ventidius works for the union of Antony and Octavia, Alexas for the union of Antony and Cleopatra). Both are also, however, instruments of division, not only because the unions they urge imply inevitable separations, but because they themselves are divided in their own natures. The one time in the play that Ventidius admits to the duelling forces within even his steadfast person affords a powerful example of the divisions and ironical crossings inherent in his support for Antony and opposition to Cleopatra:

> Ev'n I, who hate her,
> With a malignant joy behold such beauty,
> And while I curse, desire it.
>
> (IV.242-44)

His very oxymoronic expressions ("malignant joy," "curse, desire") are symptomatic of the tensions within the man. But the case of Alexas is far more severe. He is, after all, the "half-man" in the play, sometimes scheming with Cleopatra, other times with Antony. Indeed the action of the drama often pivots on his plottings and divides itself according to his schemes.

Alexas is, as several commentators have recognized, a fascinating character in his own right. Ruth Wallerstein argues that "Dryden understood Alexas more fully than he could understand Antony," and considers the development of his character "one of Dryden's finest things."[16] Miner describes Alexas as both "villain" and "a might-have-been Antony," claiming that his soliloquy on himself (III. 382-92) is "one of the great humane passages of the play."[17] Based on the way Dryden "understood" Alexas and on the empathy he often felt for him, it is tempting, I think, to view Alexas as a sort of playwright figure in *All For Love*, a director of action and controller of plot. His "fate," you will recall, meets him "at each double." It is tempting to think that Dryden's literary fate also trapped him within the confines of irreconcilable double options. If I am correct in suggesting that Dryden continually divides the structures in his play because he was consumed with the tension of opposites, then it is easy to see Alexas as his vehicle for division. Alexas's plot that Cleopatra and Dolabella make Antony jealous, for instance, results in the most severe division of the lovers, at the end of Act IV, when Antony demands:

> set all the earth
> And all the seas betwixt your sundered loves;
> View nothing common but the sun and skies.
> Now, all take several ways....
>
> (592-95)

And his plotting, in the final act, to reconcile the lovers by creating the story of Cleopatra's suicide results in the death--the ultimate separation-- of the two lovers. "She snatched her poniard," Alexas describes to Antony:

> 'Go, bear my lord,' said she, 'my last farewell,
> And ask him if he yet suspect my faith.'
> More she was saying, but death rushed betwixt.
> She half pronounced your name with her last breath,
> And buried half within her.
>
> (228-35)

In Alexas's language, too, we can see divisions--death dividing Cleopatra's final utterance, that utterance itself dividing life and death. Not surprisingly, Antony immediately doubles the implications of Alexas's story:

> Then art thou innocent, my poor dear love,
> And art thou dead?
> O those two words! their sound should be divided:
> Hadst thou been false, and died; or hadst thou lived,
> And hadst been true-- But innocence and death!
>
> (236-40)

Had their sound been divided, as Antony wishes, Cleopatra would of course be alive and innocent. And, ironically, Alexas knows that she is just that. *He* has been the instrument of division. But divisions are implicit in his nature; his reasoning in an earlier soliloquy almost justifies the contradictory results of his actions:

> She dies for love, but she has known its joys.
> Gods, is this just that I, who know no joys,
> Must die because she loves?
>
> (III.390-92)

Here is the paradoxical interplay of characters--by working for each other, they work against each other. In Alexas's case, by working for himself, he works against himself. If he is caught within a circle, both pursuing and being pursued by his fate, then our final image of him at the play's end--"Alexas bound"--seems all too appropriate. But he is bound by the world of Rome. Perhaps, if there is some connection between Alexas and Dryden, then we might also say that Dryden is similarly bound by the dictates of a literary vision that pulled him in two directions. Just as Alexas pursued one fate and was at the same time pursued by another, perhaps Dryden too was caught within a circle itself just as divided as the world of his play.

It is almost impossible to talk about oppositions of character without at the same time talking about the circular dimensions of the play. Within those dimensions, we see fates rise and fall, and continually turn on each other. Alexas's own situation, for instance, is circular in several ways. We have already seen him pursuing and fleeing his own fate, and we might rightly say that the circular fates of Antony and Cleopatra pivot on his actions: on the one hand, he brings the lovers together; on the other, he is responsible for their separation. When he bargains with Antony on behalf of Cleopatra, he presents him with a "ruby bracelet" which "may bind your arm" (II.199-200), and when Antony asks "Help me tie it" (II.218), Alexas stands ready to bring Cleopatra on the scene to complete the merger. This image of circularity takes on further associations as Ventidius reprimands Antony: "Y'are undone; / Y'are in the toils" (II.226-27). And later, when Cleopatra rewards Alexas for his compliments to her, she gives him a ring: "Take this in part of recompense. But, Oh! / I fear thou flatter'st me" (III.411-12). Even the circularity of the bribe--an exchange procedure built on the concept of balance but ultimately promoting imbalance and division--exposes the inherently contradictory forces of union and deceit.[18]

Yet these two forces are exactly what Alexas is all about. They come together best in the image of Alexas as serpent. His "half-man" nature often gives him characteristics of the reptile--creature of both land and water (recalling Serapion's witnessing of the omen--the Nile's flood and the "scaly herd" left in the water's retreat). On several occasions Alexas recalls the subtlety of Milton's Satan, scheming his way by flattery: he addresses Ventidius as "Great emperor, / In mighty arms renowned above mankind," to which the soldier replies in disgust, "Smooth sycophant!" (II.149-50, 153). And when Alexas offers the "ruby bracelet" to Antony, Ventidius warns: "Touch not these poisoned gifts" (II.203), not only paralleling Alexas with the serpent in the garden, but also Antony with Adam and of course Cleopatra with Eve. Alexas is often ready with flattery to work through others for his own victory. Antony describes him to Cleopatra as

> Your creature! one who hangs upon your smiles,
> Watches your eye to say or to unsay
> Whate'er you please! (IV.574-76)

When Alexas is "bound" at the end of the play, we see him in the confines of his own windings, meeting his fate as it has come full circle.

But this ironic fate of Alexas is also the fate of the two lovers. And for this reason I am not at all sure that the circular pattern of actions and fates indicates any sense of justice or reconcilement. Instead of meeting their proper ends (one way to understand the closing of the circle), characters seem to be increasingly confined by their circular dimensions-- circles close in on them as a vortex closes into a point, then reverses itself and moves in the opposite direction. We can see this happening in the character of Cleopatra who is alternatingly trapped and freed and then trapped again by her winding actions: she offers bracelets and rings, Octavia accuses her of spreading "snares" (III.429), Ventidius warns of her "toils" (II. 227), and Antony wishes to be captive in her "embraces" (III.18). The laurel wreath with which Cleopatra crowns Antony at the beginning of Act III is a symbol both of their union and the entrapment which Antony desires:

> I thought how those white arms would fold me in,
> And strain me close, and melt me into love;
> So pleased with that sweet image....
>
> (1-3)

If Cleopatra closes the circle around Antony, he tightens its bounds by willingly submitting. Their grand love is, ironically, tremendously confining--and that may very well be why they ultimately lose the world.

But the world, too, is merely another circle. Its bounds are no more liberating for Antony and Cleopatra than for Alexas--and Antony, when he receives the false news of Cleopatra's death, would easily give it up: "Let Caesar take the world-- / An empty circle" (V.273-74). Like most of the circles in the play, the world also has two distinct sides, as Antony goes on to bemoan, speaking of himself and Caesar:

> We two have kept its homage in suspense,
> And bent the globe, on whose each side we trod,
> Till it was dinted inwards.
>
> (V.282-84)

The circle is always divided. The laurel-wreath crown, which Cleopatra had used as a symbol of their union, turns direction and becomes a symbol of parting, one just as hollow as the "empty circle" of the world. Thus as Cleopatra prepares for her death, she commands:

> bring my crown and richest jewels;
> With 'em, the wreath of victory I made
> (Vain augury!) for him who now lies dead.
>
> (V.437-39)

56

I have been discussing circular structures in *All For Love* as paradoxical structures: they evoke the image of union, yet at the same time they contain the very seeds of division. "The Breaking of the Circle," which Marjorie Hope Nicolson associated with the seventeenth century, immediately comes to mind. In a sense, the "Circle of Perfection" was broken for Dryden. And yet I think the image of a vortex or spiral describes better the situation in *All For Love*, an image which Nicolson interestingly finds much more reflective of our modern writers:

> 'Things fall apart. The Centre cannot hold,' said Yeats, in whose poetry the circle recurs perhaps more than in that of any other English poet. His is no closed circle but a spiral in which the movement is both upward and downward.... Yeats's circle was drawn from Vico, as is that of the other modern writer who has most used it in the structure of his work, James Joyce, who said in *Finnegans Wake:* 'The Vico road goes round and round to meet where terms begin.' There may be variation but there is no progress--repetition, sometimes interruption, even degeneration. We cannot return to a world that died in the seventeenth century....[19]

I quote the passage at length because so many of Nicolson's descriptions help explain the paradox of the circle image in Dryden's play. Circles, after all, contain their own oppositions within the confines of their own circumference. And Dryden's circles, though they seem to be images of real or potential union, are rent by those inherent oppositions. The image is deceiving. At the end of *All For Love* all of the images of union are strangely subverted and, like death, "deceived by [their] own image" (V.478). Indeed the very instrument of death for Cleopatra, the aspic, becomes the culmination of all the serpent imagery previously associated with the circularity of the scheming Alexas. We can rightly appreciate the ambiguity of Cleopatra's line: "Welcome, thou kind deceiver!" (V.472). But what, exactly, is the deception?

It is the unfolding of opposites. The aspic "steals" Cleopatra from herself, changes life to death. And death will provide her with her "second spousals" (V.461), a marriage--she believes--that cannot be divided. Cleopatra's last words describe the paradoxical closing of the circle:

> O turn me to him,
> And lay me on his breast!--Caesar, thy worst.
> Now part us, if thou canst.
>
> (498-500)

We can see the images lead up to union--union in death. But the vortex, once it has closed into this point, reverses itself, and that reversal is the force of Cleopatra's final command--"O turn me to him.... Now part us, if thou canst." There is, of course, union in death. But there is, at the same time, the very threat of division inherent in that union. Cleopatra's final dare is the threatening force of division, born of the very powers of union.

The closing of the circle always seems to indicate union *and* division, a meeting at each double. We can see these bounds wrap themselves around the fate of every character. Ventidius and Antony, Octavia and Antony, Dolabella and Antony, Dolabella and Cleopatra, Antony and Cleopatra--each pair is joined through some image of union only to be finally wrenched apart, not merely by outside forces, but by the very instruments of their union. The circle is not only "broken," as Nicolson might say, by the advent of a new world view (an imposition from the outside), but also by a crumbling from within. Union reverses itself and becomes division. This is the irony of the circle image in *All For Love*, but it is an irony markedly different from the superficial contradictions of action that we normally associate with such reversals. Paul de Man's notion of the ironic comes to mind: "It obviously does not suffice to refer back to the descriptive rhetorical tradition which, from Aristotle to the eighteenth century, defines irony as 'saying one thing and meaning another.' " In terms of traditional irony, in other words, the circular image in *All For Love* would seem to mean union, but would actually mean division. Instead, as de Man goes on to say, the "dialectic of self-destruction and self-invention which ... characterizes the ironic mind is an endless process that leads to no synthesis."[20] With this notion of irony, we are left not merely observing the tragic distance between what the circle seems to be and what it clearly is not--that distance between the ideal and the real, but are left with the continuing opposition of the figurative and literal associations of this circular movement--a structure that keeps repeating itself throughout the drama. It is this kind of dualistic structure which prompts, to use de Man's words, "dizziness to the point of madness."

The ironic fate of Cleopatra is clearly a case in point. She has destroyed herself (through suicide) and reinvented herself (through her "second spousals"). But this circular movement leads to no union--unless we make the leap away from this world altogether, the world which the lovers have lost, and place our faith elsewhere--in an imagined world void of ironies. And we can see the same kind of paradoxical joinings--divisions that are unions, unions that are divisions--when the two worlds of the play merge. Serapion describes to Cleopatra the outcome of this final confrontation between Egypt and Rome:

> Cleopatra. Vanquished?
> Serapion. No.
>   They fought not.

Cleopatra. Then they fled?
Serapion. Nor that. I saw,
With Antony, your well-appointed fleet
Row out; and thrice he waved his hand on high,
And thrice with cheerful cries they shouted back.
'Twas then false Fortune, like a fawning strumpet
About to leave the bankrupt prodigal,
With a dissembled smile would kiss at parting
And flatter to the last. The well-timed oars
Now dipped from every bank, now smoothly run
To meet the foe; and soon indeed they met,
But not as foes. In few, we saw their caps
On either side thrown up; th'Egyptian galleys,
Received like friends, passed through and fell behind
The Roman rear; and now they all come forward,
And ride within the port.

(V.79-94)

Defection becomes union; foe becomes friend. And yet for Antony and Cleopatra, that very union is their ruin. Cleopatra replies, "Enough, Serapion: / I've heard my doom," and Serapion describes Antony's madness: "Withheld, he raves on you, cries he's betrayed. / Should he now find you--" (V.95, 103-4). The lovers will join again, briefly, before their deaths. Then they will separate again. The spiral continues.

And the world remains divided. The play, in its paradoxical circular structure, ends where it begins--with Serapion, Alexas, and the Priests taking the stage as they had at the opening. The omen which foretold the doom of Egypt has also come full circle, and met its own double; for the end of the play is also its beginning, and the circular fates of soldiers, wives, schemers, lovers, will all continue. "Sleep, blest pair," Serapion says, "While all the storms of fate fly o'er your tomb" (V.514-16). The drama opens with a "wild deluge" and ends with the vision of storms and disruption. Beginning is ending, and ending is beginning in this circular dramatic world, a world where the "storms of fate" are the double fates which push and pull in opposed directions. Even in their quiet unity, the "blest pair" reminds us of a world inherently divided: "See, see how th'lovers sit in state together, / As they were giving laws to half mankind!" (V. 507-8). Cleopatra's threat, "Now part us, if thou canst," strangely solidifies that vengeful division.

CHAPTER 4

Duality as Politics: Doubletalk in *Absalom and Achitophel*

"With Oaths affirm'd, with dying Vows deny'd"

When Dryden described the Jews in his *Absalom and Achitophel*, he must have found himself in a rather precarious position. The English people were, after all, "headstrong and moody," and Dryden needed somehow to account for their inconsistencies which were reflected in a series of turntable political events--the public support for Cromwell, the dismissal of his son Richard, the restoration of Charles, and finally the movement for increased parliamentary control. In one particular couplet he explains the action taken by the people when Saul (Cromwell) died and his son Ishbosheth (Richard) was forced from the throne:

> They who when *Saul* was dead, without a blow,
> Made foolish *Ishbosheth* the Crown forgo....
>
> (ll. 57-58)

The couplet prompts a dubious question. Exactly what did happen "without a blow"? Was it that Cromwell died peacefully (Saul was dead without a blow)? Or was it that the incompetent Richard was peacefully asked to abdicate (without a blow they made Ishbosheth the crown forgo)? Both actions are, of course, historically correct. Nonetheless, Dryden seems to be saying two very different things at the same time.

This is what I mean by political doubletalk. And were it not for the fact that such doubletalk appears so often in *Absalom and Achitophel*, we might excuse this instance of slippery syntax as perhaps an accidental though witty aspect of his couplet style. I see it, however, as a very calculated feature of both his style and his poetic intentions. If we think about the double meanings of this particular couplet, for instance, we might be able to see why Dryden had a very good reason for making two different statements. Dryden has, in fact, both praised and blamed the English people at the same time, praised them for not killing Cromwell, or perhaps for not murdering his son, yet implicitly blamed them for their tendency to commit such treasonous acts. The effect of this peculiar kind of doubletalk depends on the response of different readers: we might say, for instance, that the Whigs would be more prone to be amused by Dryden's witty handling of the matter of Cromwell's death, while the Tories would be more responsive to Dryden's criticism of England's political instability.

Admittedly, the range of such responses is not always easy to define, but double readings of Dryden are constantly available in his poem. In allowing for these double readings, Dryden, I believe, was demonstrating what it means to be a political poet--one who seems to support defined issues and positions, but who cleverly wavers on the details. I would further suggest that Dryden, as a political poet, had every intention to waver on issues. The very epigraph on the poem's title page, *"Si Propius Stes / Te Capiet Magis,"* is itself a sort of caution that the poem cannot be taken at face value--"the nearer you stand, the more it will seize you." Depending on your position, you can see the poem in different ways. And especially in the play of language, as I intend to show, Dryden's political statements are continually being reshaped and are continually seizing readers in different ways.

I should admit at the outset, however, that there is every reason not to think of Dryden as the kind of poet who would rely on ambivalence and doubletalk as a political mechanism, especially since we have tended to see him instead as the defender of the conservative cause. Yet his reliance on such manipulation reflects not only the double cast of his mind, but also the political atmosphere of the Restoration period itself. Dryden, we should remember, was poet laureate during an age noted for its instability and divisions. It was the first state to incorporate rival political parties into a practical system of politics. Moreover, it was a state noted for its divisions. J.R. Jones describes the political situation of Restoration England in terms of a nation "divided into hostile camps, Court against Country, then Whig against Tory, and Anglican against Dissenter."[1] We might turn to the character of King Charles himself as an example of one of the most politically divided figures of his age. A major spokesman for the Anglican faith, he was constantly suspected of being Roman Catholic. And he was continually changing his mind on nearly every major political decision of the day. Historian John Miller considers inconsistency to be Charles's defining character trait, and quotes an interesting passage from Temple's *Memoirs* on this matter:

> 'This softness of temper made him apt to fall into the persuasion of whoever had his kindness and confidence for the time, how different soever from the opinions he was of before, and he was very easy to change hands when those he

employed seemed to have engaged him in any difficulties, so as nothing looked steady in the conduct of his affairs, nor aimed at any certain end.'[2]

You will recall that Dryden himself was described in strikingly similar terms by Samuel Johnson. And it seems only appropriate that if the major political figures of the Restoration lived by a double standard, then Dryden, the major poetic spokesman of the age, should write by a double standard of expression. Dryden, I think, was well aware of the political expediency of his doubletalk.

We might consider his own comments, for instance, on his depiction of Buckingham, a portrait which Dryden himself described as "in my Opinion, worth the whole Poem."[3] Basically the portrait presents a witty characterization of a rather flamboyant character, "A man so various, that he seem'd to be, / Not one, but all Mankinds Epitome" (ll. 545-46). Indeed Zimri's imperfections are only his excesses, and much like the portrait of Charles in the opening lines of the poem, Buckingham's portrait is sketched with exaggerated and colorful strokes. Contradiction seems to be the defining charateristic of Zimri, and thus we find Dryden's language relying on oppositions: "Not one, but all," "was every thing ... and nothing," "to wish, or to enjoy," "So over Violent, or over Civil, / That every man, with him, was God or Devil." The double descriptions culminate in the final couplet of the passage where Dryden describes the way Buckingham was finally rejected by his own party:

> Thus, wicked but in will, of means bereft,
> He left not Faction, but of that was left.
>
> (ll. 567-68)

Not only are we once again presented with a series of double perspectives (Zimri is wicked in his intentions, but not in his actions; he did not leave his faction, but they left him), but we are also presented with a version of doubletalk similar to the kind Dryden used when he was speaking of Cromwell and Richard. Just as it was possible there to question what happened "without a blow," so here we might entertain two readings of the half line "of means bereft." In one sense, the message is complimentary, at least to some extent, because it implies that though Buckingham is wicked in will, he is not wicked in his means and actions (wicked in will, but bereft of the means to be wicked). Yet in a different sense, the message has much more of a bite. In the preceding lines, Dryden had been describing how Buckingham was constantly "squandring" his wealth, how "Fools" ultimately "had his Estate." Perhaps it is possible to read "of means bereft" to say that Buckingham is finally "bereft" of money (wicked in will, but bereft of any financial means to be effectively wicked). Again, political doubletalk makes two options possible, each of which might facilitate a very different kind of response--censure or sympathy.

Dryden all but acknowledges the presence of these double options when he writes in his *Discourse of Satire* his own estimation of the Zimri portrait: "'Tis not bloody, but 'tis ridiculous enough. And he for whom it was intended, was too witty to resent it as an injury. If I had rail'd, I might have suffered for it justly: But I managed my own Work more happily, perhaps more dextrously."[4] Thus the function of doubletalk. Had Dryden made a direct statement and "rail'd," he would not have attracted the political response he wanted. Instead he has chosen to handle his argument "dextrously." It was a tendency which came very naturally to him, and which also appealed very naturally to the tastes of his audience.

It is also easy to see how this double use of language, which allowed Dryden both to give the impression of clear, balanced argument and to suggest alternate arguments which prompted different meanings, might constitute an especially appropriate form of expression for this kind of poem. At the very beginning of his prefatory comments "To the Reader," Dryden admits that he is drawing "his Pen for one Party," but after emphasizing the extremes of *"Wit* and *Fool," "Whig* and *Tory,"* and "Knave" and "Ass," he concedes: "Yet if a *Poem* have a *Genius,* it will force its own reception in the World. For there's a sweetness in good Verse, which Tickles even while it Hurts: And, no man can be heartily angry with him, who pleases him against his will." Even in this series of oppositions we can see Dryden's predilection to divide his statements into double descriptions. Indeed it is not clear exactly who is the wit and who the fool, as if Dryden would prefer to blur these distinctions between Whig and Tory. And surely he does just that when he juxtaposes knave and ass, each defined only by the "contrary side." But the key political duality in this passage is the interesting opposition of "Tickles" and "Hurts." In a sense, the two responses are very similar; one simply allows for more pleasure than pain, the other more pain than pleasure. And the skillful intermixture of the two is the exact combination Dryden would need in order to praise and censure at the same time. It is also the combination, I think, that marks him as probably the best example we have of a political poet.

It was for this very reason, because he was such a political writer, that Dryden had to anticipate the vicissitudes of his audience. His portrayal of each character, whether from the loyalist or opposition camp, had to anticipate certain responses from that audience. When he deals with the king, for instance, he must accommodate both Charles's supporters and his critics, just as when he deals with the rebels he must allow, as in the case of Buckingham, some witty commentary that would make the man laugh in spite of himself. And often, as in the case of Monmouth who himself attracted strongly mixed feelings, Dryden had need to anticipate both favorable and critical responses from any one segment of his audience. This flexible handling of verse style obviously alters our conventional notion of what *Absalom and Achitophel* is all about. I would question the assumption that it is "about Charles II and his kingly office," as Bernard Schilling has argued, "showing that the man who is now king is really possessed of the qualities gathered in the conservative myth for the ideal king."[5] Instead, it is about different responses to the king, to his son, to his critics, to the entire political situation in Restoration England.

We can in fact examine the opening lines on the king as one of the outstanding examples of political doubletalk in the poem.

> In pious times, e'r Priest-craft did begin,
> Before *Polygamy* was made a sin;
> When man, on many, multiply'd his kind,
> E'r one to one was, cursedly, confin'd:
> When Nature prompted, and no law deny'd
> Promiscuous use of Concubine and Bride;
> Then, *Israel*'s Monarch, after Heaven's own heart,
> His vigorous warmth did, variously, impart
> To Wives and Slaves: And, wide as his Command,
> Scatter'd his Maker's Image through the Land.

No other lines in all of *Absalom and Achitophel* have attracted such a variety of different interpretations. Yet this diversity of response should come as no surprise. If the poem is a "Party" poem, and if Dryden supports the king and the existing political order, then why does he begin with an extended discussion of the king's promiscuity? Let me survey some of the critical interpretations of just this particular issue. Schilling claims that the question of Charles's "scandalous immorality" is "pointless and should never be raised in the first place" since Dryden deals with it through the Old Testament analogy; but Earl Miner argues that the question does indeed have a point, that Charles is "exercising his Christian liberty in scattering 'his Maker's image thro' the Land.' "[6] Then again, several other critics have taken this matter of Charles's promiscuity less seriously. Ian Jack thinks that Dryden, in being witty, employed a "masterly stroke" because to treat the issue straightforwardly would have been to invite ridicule; but Steven Zwicker sees the wit as having a different function, to establish a "witty juxtaposition of divine and human fertility." And MacDonald Emslie gives yet a different twist to such a reading by arguing that Dryden intentionally used the language of the town gentleman to increase the effect of the wit.[7] K.E. Robinson, however, is one critic who suggests an altogether different understanding of the lines, arguing that Dryden was being honest in his criticism of Charles in the beginning of the poem in order to build up to the king's "rehabilitation" at the end of the poem.[8]

What I find curious about each of these responses is that they presuppose that since Dryden was politically on the side of the king, then he must necessarily have aimed to support--somehow or another--the king's politics. But I think we can appreciate the lines more fully if we add more fullness to their context. For that purpose, let me postulate that Dryden was not aiming simply to support the king, any more than he would later in the poem simply rail at Buckingham. Instead, he begins his seemingly partisan poem by going out of his way to attract a diversity of responses.

We can find doublings appearing in the verse in a variety of ways. Consider the couplet, "When Nature prompted, and no law deny'd / Promiscuous use of Concubine and Bride." The couplet is wonderfully balanced, allowing readers to respond to a variety of associations as they mentally connect different elements of the verse. We might consider, for example, Miner's identification of "a brilliant subdued parallelism with contrast of ideas" which suggests a relationship between "Nature" and "law," and "Concubine and Bride," and also between "Nature" and "Concubine," and "law" and "Bride."[9] Miner outlines this structure in terms of the interrelationship of the following components:

nature	concubine
law	bride

Such a parallelism is surely clever enough, and we might appreciate it, as Miner does, as evidence of Dryden's mastery of the couplet form. But other kinds of doublings can also enter the picture. For instance, looking at this same couplet, we might play each half-line segment against the other and thus end up pairing what "Nature prompted" and "Promiscuous use" with "what no law deny'd" and both "Concubine and Bride." The reader's eye, in other words, might organize the couplet in this way:

nature	law
promiscuous use	concubine and bride

If Miner's observed parallelism suggests that having a concubine is natural while having a bride is legal, my observed parallelism suggests that general promiscuity is natural while having both a concubine and bride is legal. Here, then, are at least two double possibilities.

Both possibilities, of course, fit the general sense of Dryden's remarks, but the specific details of each nicely complicate the whole matter so that when we extend our thoughts to Charles and his many mistresses and his bride, we as readers can entertain various ideas about what kinds of social structures, natural and legal, support the king's relationships with mistress and wife. In one sense, a bride is legal while a mistress natural--and David (implicitly, Charles) may have both. In another sense, promiscuity is natural while having a bride/mistress is legal--and David (implicitly, Charles) may not only have both, but may also make promiscuous use of them. Whether the issue is infidelity or promiscuity, it is easy to see how the sophisticated gentleman of the town might relish the duplicities of Dryden's description.

But what of the moral dimension of the verse? Another duplicity altogether takes care of that. If a reader, for whatever reason, is disturbed by Dryden's racy tone, he need only reflect on the fact that such "pious times" are a thing of the past. Thus if Dryden's description can account for the behavior of the Biblical David, it cannot--a reader might conclude-- excuse the behavior of Charles. A reader might even see--as Robinson does--Dryden criticizing Charles in the opening lines of the poem. And it was not only the Puritan who might sense in Dryden's language an admission that different times produce different mores.

To a large extent this dual treatment of past and present, that is, statements about the past but implications about the present, is what constantly rescues Dryden from the bite of his own satire. An excellent example of how these blurred distinctions between God/David (past) and Charles (present) are enforced by Dryden's ambivalent syntax can be found in these lines:

> Then, *Israel*'s Monarch, after Heaven's own heart,
> His vigorous warmth did, variously, impart
> To Wives and Slaves....

We can see Dryden carefully setting up an analogy between *"Israel's Monarch"* (David) and God, speaking of the warmth which David imparts as being like that of "Heaven's own heart." At least, that is, we can see this particular analogy functioning in this particular way until the closure of the couplet. After that point, we discover that the analogy takes on a strikingly different meaning. We discover, in other words, that what David is really imparting is his sexual warmth. Thus the double options: David is like God (after heaven's own heart) because he imparts his vigorous warmth to everyone; and David is like God because his sexual generation resembles God's creative power. The two options are made possible by the interplay of couplet meter and syntax. The closure of the couplet enforces one reading, while the extension of syntax beyond the parameters of couplet structure enforces the other reading.

Once this kind of technical interplay is set into motion, doubles generate more doubles. For instance, there is the possible double reference of "His" in the half line "His vigorous warmth." Is it David's sexual warmth, or God's generous, creative warmth? Both the doubling of the possessive adjective reference and the doubling of the syntactic direction of the lines force us to view David as both heavenly/godlike and earthly/sexual (then Israel's monarch [David], after heaven's own heart [God], his [David's? God's?] vigorous warmth did variously impart). Or, in the half line "wide as his Command," the adjective "his" may refer either to David or God, since both rule their respective heavenly and earthly empires (his [David's? God's?] vigorous warmth did variously impart to wives and slaves, and wide as his [David's? God's?] command). In this sense, the final line, "Scatter'd his Maker's Image through the Land," evokes the perfect double image of the monarch: we can see him in terms of God's loving generosity and in terms of David's sexual generosity, censuring or praising him as we see fit.

But there is, of course, another "Monarch" whose actions complicate the whole passage--King Charles. And once again, the overlay of past times onto the present allows for a kind of double perspective that makes it possible for Dryden to talk about Charles without ever mentioning his name. Thus we have the dual (stated and implied) reference of the word "Monarch." And if we have the dual image of the monarch David as both creative and sexual, then we surely also have that same image of Charles. Finally, if we might censure or praise David accordingly, then the same is true for Charles. There is in fact every reason for Dryden to allow for both responses. In one sense, the verse is witty enough so that for the king's supporters it does little if any damage to his cause or person (indeed, the depiction may work very well to his advantage). But in another sense, for those opposed to Charles, the wit of the verse may not be enough to cover the possible criticism of Charles's actions. Thus the syntactic structure of the passage offers readers a mixture of praise, satire, and criticism. And this politically ambivalent treatment of Charles is by no means peculiar to the opening lines of the poem. Dustin Griffin has recently suggested in his study of "Dryden's Charles: The Ending of *Absalom and Achitophel*" that the exaggerated tone of the final verses undercuts what we have conventionally thought of as Dryden's serious and straightforward praise of Charles. Griffin goes on to point out Dryden's own "political expediency" in his support of the king.[10] Political doubletalk, I think, is to a large extent responsible for that expediency. It lets Dryden have things both ways, and lets his readers have things in whatever way they prefer.

Before progressing any further with a reading of the poem itself, I think it would be useful now--with some examples of doubletalk already in mind--to discuss the technical features of Dryden's couplet syntax and meter which prompt the duplicity inherent in his couplet structure. Clearly the closed heroic couplet naturally lends itself to a variety of kinds of doubling, not only in its rhyme pattern, but also in its three dominant rhetorical patterns--parallelism, juxtaposition, and antithesis.[11] Yet the plays of language which I have been discussing rely on a different aspect of couplet structure--the traditional hierarchy of half lines and lines which enforce a well-defined system of pauses, and which in turn dictate how we read couplet verse. The eighteenth-century critic John Dennis defined this system of pauses in terms of a particular kind of hierarchy. William Piper quotes Dennis, clarifying his statement in this way: " 'The Pause at the End of a Verse,' [that is, at the end of the first line] 'ought to be greater than any Pause that may precede it in the same Verse' [that is, the mid-line pause], 'and the Pause at the End of a Couplet ought to be greater than that which is at the End of the first Verse.' "[12] We might say, then, that a closed couplet is traditionally composed of four half lines, and we might envision its spatial dimension as that of four boxes, each containing a grammatical unit which typically can function both by itself and by interacting with surrounding units. Thus syntax can work in a double way.

Consider, for instance, this couplet describing one of the poem's villains:

> Yet, *Corah*, thou shalt from Oblivion pass;
> Erect thy self thou Monumental Brass.
>
> (ll. 632-33)

In terms of half lines, we automatically read the couplet as follows:

| Yet, Corah, thou shalt | from Oblivion pass |
| Erect thy self | thou Monumental Brass |

The "Monumental Brass," as most textual notes explain, alludes to the staff which Moses raised. Corah, however, must erect his own staff (you yourself erect your monumental brass). The half line "Erect thy self," in other words, is part of the larger syntactic unit of the entire line. But there is, of course, another very obvious reading embedded in the line. "Erect thy self" might function as a syntactic unit on its own, adding a different dimension to the satire, and constituting--as Paul Ramsey put it--"the most savage and most proper sexual pun Dryden ever made."[13] The line still makes sense syntactically, with "thou Monumental Brass" functioning in apposition to the first half of the line. But while one reader might appreciate the religious, or perhaps irreligious, tone of the satire, another could certainly respond to the sexual wit of the line.

Such syntactic ambivalences recall the kind of "syntactic ambiguity" that William Empson discussed briefly with reference to Dryden.[14] But Empson seemed to reject the idea that such ambiguity suited the closed couplet verse form which Dryden practiced. From the standpoint of both seventeenth-century couplet convention and twentieth-century critical theory, I think we can understand why Dryden eagerly took advantage of the interplay of syntax and meter to produce double meanings.

We know, for instance, that Dryden himself was aware of the possible different movements and functions of couplet syntax. He was once asked to clarify the grammatical construction of this couplet by Thomas Creech: "Besides, if o're whatever years prevaile / Shou'd wholly perish, & its matter faile." Dryden explained his opinion on the confusion in this way:

> The objection is, that there is no Nominative case appearing, to the word, Perish: or that can be understood to belong to it. I have considered the verses, & find the Authour of them to have notoriously bungled: that he has plac'd the words as confus'dly, as if he had studied to do so.... I pronounce therefore as impartially as I can upon the whole, That there is a Nominative case; and that figurative, so as Terence & Virgil amongst others use it. that is; the whole clause precedent is the Nominative case to perish.... If you will not admit a clause to be in construction a Nominative case; the word (thing) illud, or quodcung, is to be understood; either of which words, in the femine [sic] gender, agree with (res) so that he meanes, whatever thing time prevailes over shou'd wholly perish & its matter faile.[15]

Several of Dryden's comments indicate his own willingness to entertain different understandings of the lines. At one point, for instance, he suggests that the grammatical confusion might have been intentional-- "as if [the author] had studied to do so." And though he is willing to pronounce impartially on the matter, he allows that other syntactic options may exist--if the clause is not "in construction a Nominative case," then the understood word "thing" might function as the subject of the word "perish." There is the sense of two possibilities even in Dryden's attempt to derive a single resolution. And we should particularly keep this in mind when we remember that Dryden was called upon to settle a dispute. What is even more interesting about the situation is that though Dryden renders an opinion, or perhaps two opinions, he also accommodates the loser: "But, to comfort the looser, I am apt to believe, that the cross-grain, confused verse put him so much out of patience, that he wou'd not suspect it of any sense." Alternatives always seem to be present to Dryden. And here he also openly makes them available to his readers.

The availability of options for the reader is an aspect of Dryden's syntactic interplay that might readily be explained by contemporary criticism. When two syntactic options seem possible, then a reader will often entertain the one most suitable to him, even if it is not enforced by the surrounding syntax of the verse. As Stanley Fish explains, a reader can be suspended "between the alternatives [a line's] syntax momentarily offers."[16] In the case of Dryden's couplet, such suspension is especially momentary, that is, very quick, since the jumpy pace of the closed couplet will demand resolution often by the end of the couplet itself. And to an audience trained to respond to witty wordplay, the constant suggestion of double syntactic possibilities becomes easy to exploit. Dryden, I think, did just that. Let me now return to the poem itself to show how he sustains this technique in the depiction of different characters.

Dryden had a tendency, throughout *Absalom and Achitophel*, to treat different figures in similar ways. Having just examined his depictions of Charles and Buckingham, we might compare couplets from each portrait in order to see the double vision of hero and villain:

> Then, *Israel*'s Monarch, after Heaven's own heart,
> His vigorous warmth did, variously, impart....
>
> (ll. 7-8)

> Blest Madman, who coud every hour employ,
> With something New to wish, or to enjoy!
>
> (ll. 553-54)

The description of the carefree generosity of "*Israel*'s Monarch" who "variously" imparts his vigorous warmth throughout the land is finally very similar to the description of this "Blest Madman" who continually employs himself with actions that seem equally attractive. And the verse anticipates similar kinds of response: Dryden counts on his reader to be pleased by the description of both men, even though one technically receives his support and the other his censure. Surely Dryden is being "dextrous" in both cases, or how else would he be able to describe in such similar ways such strikingly different characters? His vision, in other words, is double: the monarch is praised, the madman is blessed. Even when comparing the opening lines on the king with Dryden's initial description of Shimei, we can see the same satiric methods at work.

> In pious times, e'r Priest-craft did begin,
> Before *Polygamy* was made a sin;
> When man, on many, multiply'd his kind,
> E'r one to one was, cursedly, confind....
>
> (ll. 1-4)

70

Shimei, whose Youth did early Promise bring
Of Zeal to God, and Hatred to his King;
Did wisely from Expensive Sins refrain,
And never broke the Sabbath, but for Gain:
Nor ever was he known an Oath to vent,
Or Curse unless against the Government.

(ll. 585-90)

If the subject matter of the two passages is different, the satiric methods and linguistic effects are nonetheless quite similar. The Shimei passage, for instance, as Schilling explains, relies on "the construction of lines and couplets that set up the anticlimaxes showing the man as odious after leading us to hope that he is better than we have thought."[17] More specifically, these "anticlimaxes" are the backlash final half lines of each couplet. But just as these final twists govern the couplet effect here, so do they in the description of the times during which *"Israel's* Monarch" reigned: once again we have the first three half lines leading to a description which the final couplet segment undercuts. Notice the three propositions, each at the beginning of a couplet block: *in* pious times, *e'r* priestcraft, *before* polygamy. It is not until the final half line, "was made a sin," that we find the completion of the syntactic sequence and the twist in meaning. And the same effect governs the progression of the next couplet. The final half line, "cursedly, confin'd," not only parallels the thought of "was made a sin," but also punctuates the couplet with backlash force. If Shimei is damned with faint praise, then the monarch is praised with faint damnation.

I am not, of course, contending that any rhetorical device--whether it be pun or oxymoron or syntactic interplay--must always produce the same effect. Clearly Slingsby Bethel suffers from the wordplay more than Charles does; that is, he is "hurt" while Charles is "tickled." But the very fact that Dryden used even these momentary double perspectives-- inducements and anticlimaxes--in depicting each character is surely evidence that for both hero and villain he relied on duplicity rather than straightforward statement. And I am also suggesting that the similarity of effect, even for these different characters, reveals more about Dryden's own political flexibility than it does about his defense of any strict political position.

Similar effects, then, can derive from descriptions of different characters. But sometimes different effects can derive from descriptions of the same character--as we saw in Dryden's initial portrait of the king, where two very different kinds of readers might understand the verse in conflicting ways. We can also find such a double perspective at work in the portrait of Achitophel, for despite the fact that Shaftesbury was the poem's chief villain, Dryden was smart enough, that is, politically

71

conscious enough, to realize the value of praising the man. Yet even when censure accommodates some praise--offering one kind of double perspective on character, that praise itself contains censure--offering a more subtle kind of double perspective. We are allowed just these two perspectives in this passage on Achitophel:

> In *Israel*s Courts ne'r sat an *Abbethdin*
> With more discerning Eyes, or Hands more clean:
> Unbrib'd, unsought, the Wretched to redress;
> Swift of Dispatch, and easie of Access.
> Oh, had he been content to serve the Crown,
> With vertues only proper to the Gown;
> Or, had the rankness of the Soyl been freed
> From Cockle, that opprest the Noble seed....

(ll. 188-95)

Notice how the half line "With vertues only" can be read as a syntactic extension of the first line of that couplet (oh had he been content to serve the crown with virtues only). We have, of course, seen this sort of syntactic extension elsewhere in the verse. Once it is put into play, succeeding half lines and lines become altered in their meaning. When read in this way, for instance, the remaining half line "proper to the Gown" can take on a double reference: it can refer to "he" in the preceding line, suggesting that he, Achitophel, might have been proper to the gown; or it can refer to "vertues" in the preceding half line, suggesting that it was the virtues rather than the man that were actually appropriate to the gown. The situation is complicated by the possible double reference of the word "only": couplet meter, which calls for a mid-line pause after "only," links the word with "vertues" (Achitophel should have been content to serve the crown only with virtues). But if syntax runs counter to meter--as it often does in Dryden--the word "only" may modify "proper," and we would be forced to distinguish between only virtues, only proper virtues, and virtues proper only to the gown. What, then, does Dryden exactly mean when he says that Shaftesbury should have been content to serve the crown? And how might Shaftesbury have acted in this way: by following his own sense of virtue which accorded with the law, or perhaps by acting only with virtue and not the vice which implicitly came naturally to him? Dryden's particular message here is obviously ambivalent, even in spite of the fact that his general treatment of Shaftesbury is so straightforwardly critical. Like Bethel, Shaftesbury is not saved by the double perspective: he still comes out the victim of Dryden's satire. But like the king, Shaftesbury is nonetheless allowed salvation in another time: just as the "pious times" provided a much better context for Charles's behavior, so past times have witnessed much better conduct of Shaftesbury. And yet even with this admission, the double standard is still at work: perhaps those pious times, as some moralists might argue, were not so pious after all; and perhaps Shaftesbury's former behavior, as some of his enemies might argue, was not so wholesome even then.

Because *Absalom and Achitophel* is a "Party Poem," it naturally has its heroes and villains. But the character of Absalom does not fit conveniently into either category. Dryden seems particularly eager to maintain a sense of ambivalence about Monmouth, insisting in his prefatory comments "To the Reader" that the rift between father and son, king and rebel, might still be mended. And Dryden's reasons for blurring the line are all too clear: Monmouth was not only admired by many of the English people, but was also the object of his father's affections. If dexterity was ever to serve Dryden well, it would in the portrait of Absalom. Here Dryden was walking the line. He could not offer direct praise, yet neither could he afford to disenfranchise either the king or the people by being overly critical of the young man. That is why, of course, Absalom--not evil enough on his own--is tempted into rebellion by Achitophel. And that is also why Dryden, in his portrait of Absalom, exploited the interplay of syntax and meter more subtly here than anywhere else in the poem:

> Of all this Numerous Progeny was none
> So Beautifull, so brave as *Absolon:*
> Whether, inspir'd by some diviner Lust,
> His Father got him with a greater Gust;
> Or that his Conscious destiny made way
> By manly beauty to Imperiall sway.
> Early in Foreign fields he won Renown,
> With Kings and States ally'd to *Israel's* Crown:
> In Peace the thoughts of War he coud remove,
> And seem'd as he were only born for love.
> What e'r he did was done with so much ease,
> In him alone, 'twas Natural to please.
> His motions all accompanied with grace;
> And *Paradise* was open'd in his face.
>
> (ll. 17-30)

The third line, "Whether inspir'd by some diviner Lust," can either complete the thought of the preceding line (Absalom has been inspired by some diviner lust), or initiate the thought of the following line (David has been inspired by some diviner lust). With each reading--one an expectation, the other a confirmation--the meaning of divine lust becomes notably changed. For Absalom, such divine lust could refer to his general robust cast--his beauty and bravery, his desire for renown and military victory. For David, lust clearly refers to sexuality--his divine lust and greater gust give shape to the couplet. With the first reading, we expect that Dryden is going to compliment Absalom; with the second reading, the complimentary tone shifts both substance and reference. Syntax has thus led us to anticipate something that we do not finally get. Yet, unlike the kind of anticlimaxes enforced by metrical half lines in the Shimei passage, or even in the opening verses on the king, the effect prompted by syntactic expectancy in these lines on Absalom is far more subtle. Dryden's praise of Monmouth is so intricately tied to his praise of the king, "His Father," that it becomes almost impossible for a reader to credit Absalom with anything more than what his father has made of him. Surely Charles and those who sympathized with him would want to read the verse in this way, though at the same time Monmouth's supporters can appreciate Dryden's apparently pure praise for the young man. The double vision in part helps sustain the wit of the lines, but in part it serves Dryden's political purposes quite nicely.

As we continue to read the passage, however, humorous wit gives way to a more serious form of wordplay. In the couplet "Early in Foreign fields he won Renown, / With Kings and States ally'd to *Israel*'s Crown," the pauses enforced by meter and syntax isolate half-line units which complicate the question of Absalom's alliances. When the verse is read in sequence, it seems as though the "Kings and States" are the ones "ally'd to *Israel*'s Crown" (with kings and states which were allied to Israel's crown). But the parallel relationship between each half line--"he won Renown," "ally'd to *Israel*'s Crown"--suggests that it is Absalom who is the one allied to the crown (he won renown while allied to Israel's crown). Understanding the verse in this way only serves to highlight the fact that Absalom has clearly changed his alliances. Indeed we can sense in Dryden's tone here the same kind of double perspective that he would later apply to Achitophel: had Absalom only been content to remain allied to the crown, as had Achitophel only remained content to serve the crown, then the political situation in which England found itself would be so different. From one perspective we can see the qualities of these two men reflected in their possibilities; from another perspective, we see their flaws reflected in their actions. And to Dryden, of course, it was politically expedient to give us the double perspective.

In both of the examples I have just discussed there is yet another kind of double perspective which Dryden presents--a distinction between the causes and effects of Absalom's character and situation. In the first example, we initially think that Absalom's beauty and bravery are caused by some divine inspiration, only to discover finally that it is the king, not the son, who is responsible for the young man's qualities. And in the second example, we initially believe that Absalom's renown derives from his association with kings and states who are allied to the crown, only to discover that what Dryden may be saying is that Absalom's renown actually derives from his opposition to the crown. This same kind of confusion about what causes what is also supported by the structure of the first four couplets of the passage. The two middle couplets,

> Whether, inspir'd by some diviner Lust,
> His Father got him with a greater Gust;
> Or that his Conscious destiny made way
> By manly beauty to Imperiall sway,

all constitute one subordinate clause which falls directly in the middle of a four-couplet main clause. Yet the subordinate clause can move in two directions, modifying either the first or fourth couplet. If it modifies the first, then we might understand the subordinate clause to explain why Absalom is so beautiful and brave; but if it modifies the fourth, then we can only understand it to explain why Absalom was able to win renown. Once again, double perspectives are doubled even further. Not only are we able to understand the main clause-couplets in different ways, but also the modifications enforced by peripheral comment. On a technical level, syntax becomes web-like in its metrical structure, weaving together a whole complex of argument with the supracouplet structure of the verse. On a semantic level, the double syntax enforces again distinctions between cause and effect. Did his father's divine lust cause his beauty and bravery? Or did his own conscious destiny cause them? Or, is it that his conscious destiny caused his renown? Or, is his father's divine lust responsible for that, too?

Questions such as these are suggested throughout the entire passage on Absalom, constantly casting shadows and doubts on everything Dryden says about the young man. Each of the final three couplets sustains this ambivalent treatment of character, each in a slightly different way. When Dryden writes, for instance, "In Peace the thoughts of War he coud remove, / And seem'd as he were only born for love," we might wonder exactly what Dryden means. Christopher Ricks is at least one observer who has noted what he calls the "scepticism in 'And seem'd as he were only born for love'; first, seem'd; and second, the puns in 'for love' (because David made love; to make love; to be loved)."[18] I might add that couplet syntax enforces these ironies of diction by framing the puns within the final half line "were only born for love." In the previous couplet, Dryden had used the final half line, "ally'd to Israel's Crown," for a very similar effect. And in the couplet which follows, he again relies on the final half line to undercut the favorable tone of the verse: "What e'r he did was done with so much ease, / In him alone, 'twas Natural to please." We might ask whether it was natural for Absalom to be pleased, or natural for him to be so pleasing to others. And if we do entertain the

75

possibility that Dryden is here talking about Absalom's ability to please his followers, then we can more easily account for Dryden's emphasis elsewhere on the deception inherent in Absalom's character, something he hints at in the final couplet of the passage when he describes how *"Paradise* was open'd in his face." But then again, exactly what does this allusion mean? Schilling suggests that Dryden is actually being critical of Monmouth: "The more attractive he was, the easier the deception of those who must be deceived. His beauty suggests the surface charm of the illusions leading to rebellion."[19] Perhaps--and yet Dryden is remarkably gracious in his implied censure. If we can pick up on the deception which Dryden finds in Monmouth, it is only because we experience the description of beauty and bravery first. That is what the verse actually tells us. The deception is always suggested.

Criticism of the Absalom passage has typically relied on what the verse suggests rather than what it actually says, since the direct statements which Dryden makes are apparently not in line with the views he should be expressing about Monmouth.[20] But why would Dryden have gone out of his way to give this favorable impression of the young man unless he anticipated that a large element of his audience would in fact respond positively to these favorable impressions? And why would he likewise have suggested and implied all sorts of unfavorable things about Absalom's character unless he anticipated different responses from different kinds of readers, or even ambivalent responses from the same group of readers? Questions such as these make me suspect not only the straightforwardness of Dryden's statements, but of his entire political outlook as well. His poetic treatment of character and situation, to a greater or lesser degree, seems consistently to validate the statement he made in his prefatory remarks: "And every man is a Knave or an Ass to the contrary side." With doubletalk, Dryden is always giving us those contrary sides.

Though I have been focusing on a very specific kind of doubletalk in the poem, dualities and contraries are by no means restricted to its peculiar linguistic dimensions. We can find schemes of equivocation everywhere. Sometimes oppositions are inherent in the very nature of Dryden's subject, and we find the poet himself making contradictory statements: "And Peace it self is War in Masquerade" (l. 752); "In midst of health Imagine a desease" (l. 756). Sometimes the oppositions are part of the double response Dryden anticipates from his readers, as when he describes schemes for the "Plot": "To please the Fools, and puzzle all the Wise" (l. 115); "Believing nothing, or believing all" (l. 117). In this category we might consider the double response of the king to his son: "What faults he had (for who from faults is free?) / His Father coud not, or he woud not see" (ll. 35-36). On other occasions Dryden will divide certain situations and characters, apparently for no stronger reason than that the tendency to divide and duplicate came very naturally to him. When he speaks of the Jebusites, for instance, he describes how "Their Taxes doubled as they lost their Land" (l. 95). Or when he describes the combination of wit and madness in Achitophel, he speaks of "thin Partitions" which "their Bounds divide" (l. 164).

What of course also came very naturally to Dryden were parallel and antithetical rhetorical structures. Of the loyal Barzillai he writes: "The Court he practis'd, not the Courtier's art: / Large was his Wealth, but larger was his Heart" (ll. 825-26). Dryden also used the same see-saw rhetoric to describe Zimri. And we can see him using it in the portrayal of the rebel Shimei: "Cool was his Kitchen, tho his Brains were hot" (l. 621). But this tendency of Dryden, though it might have been no more than an easy rhetorical predilection at times, also served him quite well at other times. At the end of the poem, for instance, Dryden has David explain the predicament and fate of the rebels first in terms of a front-back duality ("They coud not be content to look on Grace, / Her hinder parts, but with a daring Eye / To tempt the terror of her Front, and Dye," ll. 1007-9), and later in terms of elements that double upon themselves ("Thus on my Foes, my Foes shall do me Right," l. 1017). And not surprisingly, the king finally threatens to rise upon the rebels "with redoubled might" (l. 1023).

Yet if the opposed elements of Dryden's dualities are obvious, the side which Dryden stands on is not. The dynamics of his dualities require pivotal positions: we can see things only from certain vantage points, and indeed the closer we stand--as Dryden has told us--the more the poem will seize us. When Dryden does pull us away, give us some distance, then we can focus on the dualities as dualities. In this way he allows us a double vision of the "Plot," ostensibly the "Popish Plot," but surely also the plot of Achitophel and Absalom:

> Rais'd in extremes, and in extremes decry'd;
> With Oaths affirm'd, with dying Vows deny'd.
>
> (ll. 110-11)

Dryden knew only too well the potential value or damage, depending on one's perspective, of both political "extremes" in Restoration England. But he also knew that "Polititians neither love nor hate" (l. 223), a line which he appropriately uses to describe Achitophel, the master politician in the poem. Instead politicians waver, using whatever means available so that they can "always cheat and always please" (l. 748). Perhaps Achitophel exerted that kind of control at one point in the poem. Perhaps David exerted the control at another point. But they may only be knaves and asses to the contrary side. If, on the other hand, Dryden controls perspective--allowing his language to seize us in different ways--then he is the one who can cheat and please for political purposes. He is the real master politician in the poem.

CHAPTER 5

Duality as Dismissal: The Uncertainties of *Religio Laici*

"Both parts *talk* loudly, but the *Rule* is *mute"*

Dryden was not a profound religious poet, at least not in the sense that Milton and Donne were. We rarely see him caught up in the torment of faith and doubt, but instead always seem to find him on the surface of religious controversy. Especially in his *Religio Laici*, his statements are rarely personal, and almost always public. It might be safe to say that Dryden never impresses with his religious feeling, but always with his religious discourse. And it was very likely this predilection to stay on the whirlwind surface of religious controversy that eventually caused him so much trouble with his critics. For the fact is that Dryden went back and forth, if not in his religious beliefs, then certainly in his discourse. Perhaps, as Johnson might say, that kind of vacillation was simply the result of Dryden's fondness for throwing himself into both sides of issues. But whatever the cause, the vacillation itself was cause enough to cast suspicion on the poet's religious statements.

Writing near the close of the nineteenth century, Alexandre Beljame, for instance, offers a very typical criticism of Dryden when he explains the poet's "bogus conversion" to Catholicism "for material advantage." He concludes with a matter-of-fact question and answer: "Had Dryden made himself conspicuous by strength of character? Far from it. In politics as in religion his convictions were fluid."[1] Such a view is, of course, dated, mainly because it explains Dryden's religious change from Anglicanism to Catholicism as the result of the poet's need "to make a living by his pen." We have long since disproved the notion that Dryden changed his religion for actual monetary compensation, but the more general notion that he was somewhat expedient when it came to religious matters is by no means dead. William Empson's explanation of Dryden's conversion comes to mind:

> He decided he had reached an age when he had better make
> solid legal arrangements to escape Hell; now an Anglican

God would accept a Papist, but not a Papist God an Anglican. He would think the Court of Heaven as very like the Court of a Stuart.[2]

The problem with such statements is that they make Dryden seem a bit unrespectable as a religious thinker, not to mention the shadows they cast on his political loyalties. But it wasn't simply the change from Anglicanism to Catholicism that raised suspicions. It was the way Dryden handled his religious discourse--the way he took hold of an issue, played with it, and then let it go. It was the way he left his reader unsure about exactly what had been argued and who had finally won the argument.

Johnson reminds us that Dryden loved to engage in disputation, and surely Dryden's religious poems are some of the best examples of the dynamics of disputation. But I do not see Dryden as ever having resolved these religious arguments which he continually set forth. He was far more satisfied with the actual process of debate and argument than he was with resolution and conclusion. That is what I mean by duality as dismissal: Dryden obviously loved to engage in the two-sidedness of religious issues, yet he was also very willing to leave those issues unsettled--something which he does very consciously in his *Religio Laici*, the particular poem I want to examine.

I choose this poem not only because, as one critic says, it is "the work central to all major studies of Dryden's religious positions,"[3] but also because it is so obviously a very confusing work. Critics have nearly always approached it as a problem--a sort of puzzle which needs to be solved. We often hear of the poem's main subjects described as oxymoronic, paradoxical, and even contradictory.[4] Moreover, we often see the poem treated in terms of dual structures: the major two-part division of the discourse itself, the vacillation of subject matter--what one critic called the poem's "dialectic of ideas," and the apparent middle position Dryden assumes between two extreme positions.[5] Indeed, *Religio Laici* has a particularly interesting critical history, in part because of the disagreement about its meaning, and in part because that disagreement reflects the religious debate contained within the poem itself. As a result of this close relationship between critical and poetic argument, a review of the criticism devoted to *Religio Laici* becomes a curious sort of commentary on the very issues which Dryden raises in his poetic discourse.

These critical/poetic arguments revolve around several different subjects, the most important of which include Reason and Scripture, Father Simon's *Critical History of the Old Testament* and Henry Dickinson's translation of that work, and the various religious systems associated with Deists, Catholics, Anglicans, and Sectarians. In an attempt to make sense of the interplay of these subjects--that is, to discover exactly what Dryden is arguing, why he is proceeding in a certain fashion, and where he finally stands--various critical arguments have been superimposed upon the poem. Each proposes a method for understanding the poem's argument, and usually this method reflects both historical context and textual interpretation. Each, in other words, creates a certain "strategy" for *Religio Laici*,[6] suggesting sources of influence for Dryden's statements and reasons for his "intentional" poetic strategy.

The outlines of these critical/poetical arguments are well known to Dryden scholars. Louis Bredvold's thesis that Dryden was a skeptic and a fideist who naturally turned to the authority of the Catholic Church was an argument that made perfect sense to scholars for nearly thirty years. After all, it explained why Dryden was so vehement in attacking the Deists in the first half of the poem, it separated him as well from the rationalistic tendencies of seventeenth-century Anglican leaders, and finally it solved the problem of his conversion to Catholicism.[7] Accounting for Dryden's conversion to Catholicism was, in fact, one of the major achievements of Bredvold's strategy since it successfully answered charges about the insincerity and opportunism of Dryden's turn to the Catholic church. But if the strategy made Dryden into a respectable Catholic, it made *Religio Laici* --a poem which he wrote when he himself was a firm Anglican--into a very suspect Anglican treatise. And that is precisely the issue which eventually caused a complete change in our approach to both the poem and Dryden's religious convictions.

Nearly thirty years after Bredvold's claim, critics began to explore the Anglican dimensions of *Religio Laici*. In particular, two books appeared which offered totally different strategies for the poem. Phillip Harth's thorough study of possible "contexts" for Dryden's religious thought redefined the nature of the poet's skepticism--dissociating him from the fideism of Montaigne and aligning him with the positive skeptical thought of Bacon and the new science. Moreover, Harth finds Dryden's religious expression in *Religio Laici* to be remarkably in tune with Anglican apologetics: both the poet's attack on the Deists and the middle position he assumes between the extremes of Catholics and Sectarians reflect the "Anglican *via media.*"[8] Sanford Budick, though disagreeing with Harth on several points, nonetheless added weight to this revised strategy for understanding *Religio Laici* by exploring the influence of the Cambridge Platonists on Dryden. Showing that Dryden was very much a rationalist himself, Budick argues that the progress of *Religio Laici* is to redefine the proper function of reason as "reformed private reason" which ultimately leads to "sacred truth."[9] Once again, the strategy fit the poem which, as it turned out, proved to be just as accommodating to an Anglican as well as Catholic perspective.

The only other book-length study of Dryden's religious thought appeared ten years later. G. Douglas Atkins, in *The Faith of John Dryden*, assumed a somewhat different perspective on the subject. Instead of approaching *Religio Laici* in terms of its Catholic or Anglican contexts, Atkins focuses on the "specifically lay approach to religion" which the poem offers. Indeed Dryden's opposition to the Anglican clergy and particularly to the impure religious practices of the Latitudinarians (with whom, Atkins argues, Dryden has been mistakenly associated) can be seen as instrumental in his eventual turn to the pure religion of both the Catholic clergy and Catholic faith.[10] *Religio Laici*, according to this critical strategy, becomes a poem with an "unresolved conflict" between layman and clergy--and the *via media* which it presents is but a "tenuous" compromise which Dryden will ultimately come to reject.

If we pause to consider the general outlines of these three critical strategies which have been superimposed upon the poem, it becomes clear that each of them treats *Religio Laici* not merely in terms of its problematic argument, but specifically in terms of a two-sided conflict.[11] For Bredvold, the poem addresses the conflict between Rationalism and Fideism, an opposition which eventually leads Dryden to reject the power of Reason and accept the Catholic faith. For Harth and Budick, *Religio Laici* presents the conflict between Deist and Anglican, between the delusion of pure Reason and the modified rationalism of Anglican apologetics. For Atkins, the poem shows a conflict between clergy and layman, exposes the grounds for Dryden's rejection of both Deism and Anglican rationalism, and finally shows his reliance on the simple faith of the layman. The two-fold dimension of each critical strategy, it seems to me, reflects the relationship between critical and poetic argument. Critics, in other words, inevitably treat the poem in terms of a two-sided conflict because the poem itself is so obviously constructed around double issues. What I want to investigate is this double poetic strategy which Dryden adopted, for I am willing to argue that his entire approach to the writing of *Religio Laici* involved a markedly dualistic strategy which relied on the interplay of opposed views that eventually cancelled each other out.

Obviously I am treating *Religio Laici* as a poem not very different from Dryden's other verse, as a poem which reflects the same kinds of double thrusts that we saw, for instance, in *Absalom and Achitophel*. That poem involved a subtle political strategy which relied on "doubletalk," a linguistic vehicle allowing Dryden to bargain with political issues. *Religio Laici*, it seems to me, also has a very definite strategy of its own, one that allows Dryden to bargain with religious issues. I believe that Empson was all too accurate in suggesting that Dryden would approach the "Court of Heaven" in much the same way as he would the "Court of a Stuart." In fact, Dryden's own discussion of various religious bargains in the poem, as well as his own bargaining strategy in adopting the layman's position, can tell us much about how he handled religious discourse and what he himself was bargaining for in the poem.

What I want to examine, then, and what I take to be Dryden's own two-fold strategy in *Religio Laici*, is the bargaining procedure in the discourse--a procedure that I will be referring to as the metaphor of exchange. The metaphor served Dryden nicely because it probably explained best his own notion of religion: the contract between God and man, what we must pay here on earth (the "price") in order to please God and secure everlasting happiness in heaven (the "gain"). That process of exchange is probably best revealed through Dryden's reliance on the word "Interest," a word which carried both financial and religious meaning. In a passage which falls at the very center of *Religio Laici* --in the midst of Dryden's commentary on Dickinson's translation and on Simon's treatise itself--Dryden describes what one critic calls "the real significance of the *Critical History* ... its apparently unintentional but accurate testimony to the ways in which certain 'Interests' appear prominently in the transmission of Scripture."[12] The issue is, of course, a pivotal one in the poem since Simon's treatise--which Dryden comments on here--has called into question the reliability of scripture. The passage reads as follows:

> Where we may see what *Errours* have been made
> Both in the *Copiers* and *Translaters Trade:*
> How *Jewish, Popish,* Interests have prevail'd,
> And where *Infallibility* has *fail'd.*
>
> (ll. 248-51)

The surface meaning seems obvious: we cannot rely on the Old Testament because of errors in the process of transmission and because of warring interests on the part of those who disseminate the scriptural word. But what I find curious is another possible meaning of the word "Interests," a meaning which corresponds to the kinds of bargains that we find in the poem. It is the meaning of interest as exchange, more particularly, of interest as the trades we make when we cannot find a truly equitable means of exchange. In the context of the poem, then, "Interests" would be the very language we bargain with as a means to gain religious understanding. But it is a language, as we will see later, that is never sufficient to its end--it inevitably implies a sense of imbalance and inequity. And what Dryden's layman must learn, what Dryden indeed discovers for himself, is that he has to live with that imbalance, with that uncertainty.

In focusing on the notion of "Interest," as well as on the kinds of bargains and exchanges which occur in the poem, I am of course referring in part to what is commonly recognized as the commercial imagery in *Religio Laici*. MacDonald Emslie and Arthur Hoffman were the first to devote some attention to this so-called image pattern, each critic seeing the images serving some technical function in the poem. Hoffman, for instance, argues that the commercial imagery "presents the mean departures from and venal corruptions of the relationship rendered initially in the borrowing of light lent from above until the advent of *Day's bright Lord*."[13] And Stanford Budick, who devotes perhaps the fullest attention to an explication of these images, ties them in very closely with his argument about Dryden's view of Reason in the poem. Budick, you will remember, argued that *Religio Laici* insists on the need to redefine the Deistic notion of Reason so that both rationalism and revelation can serve as a means to gain religious understanding. Since Dryden, according to Budick, applies the "full weight of the commercial metaphor" to Catholics and Sectarians, he therefore uses his commercial imagery to show "the need for reforming the materialistic mode of human reason."[14]

Both kinds of critical perspectives on the poem's commercial metaphor seem to me to be valid. But I am not sure that the function of the images is simply to highlight some religious message in the poem. And that is why I would prefer to treat them as reflective of Dryden's double poetic strategy in his writing of the poem. It is a strategy, as we will see, that defines not only the idiom Dryden uses to treat the dual nature of various religious systems, but one which explains his own dual approach to religious discourse.

Let us look, first, at the specific metaphors of exchange that we find in the depiction of the Deists. In the midst of Dryden's argument with the Deist, we are told that these believers in the power of reason subscribe to some fundamental *"Rules* of Worship" which are "Distributed alike to all by Heaven" (ll. 46-47). These rules Dryden calls the "Means," and they are divided into two parts:

> This *general Worship* is to *PRAISE*, and *PRAY:*
> One part to *borrow* Blessings, one to *pay*....
>
> (ll. 50-51)

It is not clear whether the couplet relies on a simple parallel relationship between the two lines (linking praise with borrowing, and prayer with payment) or on the rhetorical structure of chiasmus (linking prayer with borrowing, and praise with payment). But either way, the bargain defines the Deist's means to contract with God, much as if God were a banker who had distributed among us certificates of deposit and withdrawal. Once the Deist subscribes to these "Means," he must then be concerned with the "Effects" which, unlike the means, are not distributed equitably, but are instead "variously dispens'd" (ll. 49-55). Because of the discontinuity between means and effects (because, in other words, praise and prayer sometimes fail to produce their desired end-- *"Vice Triumphs, and Vertue suffers here,"* l. 56), the Deist then reasons that there must be a *"future* State" where all accounts are balanced--"the *Bad* meet *Punishment,* the *Good, Reward"* (l. 61).

Now Dryden proceeds to explain why this Deistic *"Systeme"* "built on *"Pray'r* and *Praise"* (ll. 82-83) is inadequate. His objection rests on several arguments, each of which also relies on the exchange metaphor. For one thing, the *"Systeme"* does not allow for "Remorse" and penitence; instead, it forces us to the terms of a "Bribe" which promises justice in the end: "Nor did Remorse, to Expiate Sin, prescribe: / But slew their fellow Creatures for a Bribe" (ll. 85-86). Moreover, the nature of the bribe itself makes atonement (payment) all too easy for some: "If *Sheep* and *Oxen* cou'd Attone for Men / Ah! at how cheap a rate the *Rich* might Sin!" (ll. 89-90). Nor do the terms of the Deist's contract take into account God's mercy:

> Look humbly upward, see his Will disclose,
> The *Forfeit first,* and then the *Fine* impose:
> A *Mulct thy* Poverty cou'd never pay
> Had not *Eternal Wisedom* found the way
> And with Coelestial Wealth supply'd thy Store:
> *His Justice* makes the *Fine, his* Mercy quits the *Score.*
> (ll. 101-6)

The only payment that can truly atone for man's sins is payment of an equal kind: since the sin was against God, the payment must be godlike. And the Deist, Dryden argues, also fails to take this fact--the fact of Christ's sacrifice for man's sins--into account:

> Some Price, that bears *proportion,* must be paid;
> And *Infinite* with *Infinite* be weigh'd.
> See then the *Deist lost : Remorse* for *Vice,*
> *Not* paid, or *paid, inadequate* in price....
> (ll. 113-16)

The Deist's contract, the "Bribe" by which he lives, is clearly unbalanced. Our debt to God is too great; payment is impossible. Thus the two-fold bargain of prayer and praise, of borrowing and payment, is simply not sufficient to its end--heavenly justice. Even the Deist's vehicle of understanding, his reason, is compared to the "borrow'd beams of Moon and Stars" in the very first line of the poem, as if to let us know from the outset that the bargainings of reason are inadequate.

Religio Laici opens, then, not merely with the notion of borrowing, but with an extended attack on Deism--an attack saturated with references to contracts and exchanges. Dryden, in other words, immediately adopts a two-fold strategy of bargaining for his religious discourse. Had he not returned to the metaphor later in the poem--especially in his description of the Catholics and to a lesser extent in his portrayal of the Sectarians-- the metaphor might have functioned well enough as a way to describe the materialistic nature of the Deistic religious system. But, as we will see, Dryden is obviously just as willing to rely on the metaphor for his description of extremely spiritual religions as well.

For the Catholics, the nature of the "Bribe" is very different. The Deist's contract is between God and man; the Catholic's contract is between the church and the people. The contract itself provides the Catholic church with its "gainfull Trade," and the transactions made between clergy and layman result in a bribe as grossly unbalanced as that of the Deist:

> Then *Mother Church* did mightily prevail:
> She parcel'd out the Bible by *retail:*
> But still *expounded* what She *sold* or *gave;*
> To keep it in *her Power* to *Damn* and *Save:*
> *Scripture* was *scarce,* and as the Market went,
> Poor *Laymen* took *Salvation* on *Content;*
> As needy men take Money, good or bad:
> *God's* Word they had not, but the *Priests* they had.
> Yet, whate'er *false Conveyances* they made,
> The *Lawyer* still was *certain* to be paid.
>
> (ll. 376-85)

Like the Deist, the Catholic tips the scales to his own advantage, awarding himself the *"Power* to *Damn* and *Save."* Clearly it is a "gainfull Trade" for the Catholics since, on the other side of the scale, we find the "Poor *Laymen*" described as "needy men" who will take whatever they can get. Even if some *"false Conveyances"* are made, the *"Lawyer,"* that is, the priest, still receives payment.

But worse yet, this imbalance only serves to engender another. For when "the written Word" is finally *"produc'd,"* the layman then realizes how he has been *"cheated"* (ll. 392-93). The contract, now in the hands of the Sectarians, becomes drastically expanded:

> Then, every man who saw the Title fair,
> Claim'd a Child's part, and put in for a Share:
> Consulted Soberly his private good;
> And sav'd himself as cheap as e'er he cou'd.
>
> (ll. 394-97)

Heaven now becomes a stock market, but one very different from the "Market" of the Catholics. For now all bargaining is conducted between each individual and God, between each shareholder and the director of the "Coelestial Wealth." Indeed, the whole "Systeme" of exchange becomes inverted: instead of engaging in a "gainfull Trade" by parcelling out the Bible "by retail," each sectarian is now "of *his Trade*, and of the *Bible free*," and instead of Scripture supplying some sort of profit, it "turns to *Maggots* what was meant for *Food*" (ll. 408, 420).

If we trace the development of Dryden's exchange metaphor in his depiction of Deist, Catholic, and Sectarian, we can see very different kinds of bargains occurring--all notably inadequate because they fail to fulfill the terms of a balanced contract. But the pivotal question, it seems to me, is why would Dryden have relied on the notion of unbalanced contracts for his description of each different religious system? Why, in other words, did he use that specific metaphor at all?

The answer I would suggest is that the notion of contract provided Dryden with the dual dimensions of his subject, dualities which he will finally be content to leave unreconciled. His own playfulness with the arguments (and indeed he used the word "play" to describe the whole "Question" under debate, l. 321) shows us a poet who is interested not only in the double sides of a series of financial accounts, but in the ways in which each imbalance engenders other contracts just as inadequate as the original. Like Hobbes and his self-perpetuating system of oppositions, Dryden intensifies the oppositions inherent in the different brands of religious thought by multiplying them. The exchange metaphor, in other words, suited his dualistic approach to the subject: it allowed him to pose opposites next to each other, and at the same time expose their irreconcilable nature.

Of course the notion of bargaining was by no means new to Dryden. He had used it in *All For Love*, with Cleopatra constantly extending bribes and payment for services. And he had used it also in *Absalom and Achitophel*, notably in his description of the Catholics ("Their Taxes doubled as they lost their Land"--yet another failed contract). And he continued to use the metaphor later in his career. We can find it on several occasions in *The Hind and the Panther*.[15] To me, one of the most interesting employments of this bargaining process appears in another poem with a religious context, Dryden's "Prologue to *Don Sebastian*," written after his own conversion to Catholicism when he himself suffered from those "double taxes" wittily described in his political poem.

The entire prologue is filled with the language of bargaining. Dryden "Petitions" his audience for their graces, trying to "bribe" them in much the same fashion as young ladies bribe legislators (another merging of religion and politics). The terms of this bargain are simple: "Sign but his Peace, he vows he'll ne'er again / The sacred Names of Fops and Beau's profane" (ll. 34-35). But what is particularly interesting is the way Dryden works the subject of religion into this literary bargain. His old contract with the public has expired; he is now a Catholic poet in a Protestant nation. But having reminded his audience that "a Play's of no Religion" (l. 16), he proposes a new contract based on his Catholicism:

> Horses, by Papists are not to be ridden;
> But sure the Muses Horse was ne'er forbidden.
> For in no Rate-Book, it was ever found
> That *Pegasus* was valued at Five-pound:
> Fine him to daily Drudging and Inditing;
> And let him pay his Taxes out, in Writing.

(ll. 41-46)

The prologue was delivered in 1689, seven years after Dryden had debated very different kinds of bargains in his *Religio Laici*. Yet even this exchange--the offer to pay taxes out in writing--is unbalanced in its very nature, and Dryden's tone is sufficiently sarcastic.

The very fact that inadequate exchanges and unbalanced contracts were so much a part of Dryden's poetic idiom makes it very likely that his reliance on the metaphor in *Religio Laici* says more about himself than about the particular religious issues he discusses in that poem. On the other hand, his extensive and systematic use of the metaphor in *Religio Laici* does indeed say something about how he worked dualisms into a specifically religious discourse. The metaphor of exchange, in other words, was certainly a part of his poetic language in this poem, just as it was also a part of Dryden's entire poetic outlook.

I suggested earlier that this metaphor defines a two-fold poetic strategy in *Religio Laici*, and that both metaphor and strategy help explain how Dryden handled his religious discourse and what he himself was bargaining for. The answer to the first issue--how Dryden approached his discourse--seems clear enough. He considered it in terms of a series of religious contracts, double sides of wagers, which were inevitably unbalanced. This is the way Dryden discusses religious duality. Where he himself stands in the midst of these exchanges brings us to a consideration of the second issue. What exactly was Dryden bargaining for?

I think that he was bargaining for a way out of the contradictory "Means" and "Effects" of each religious group. But I do not think he ever found it. For one thing, Dryden was too content with the bargaining procedure itself. For another, he continually found that any apparent reconciliation was, upon further examination, just as inadequate as the original contract. Throughout *Religio Laici*, Dryden is always proposing answers and then withdrawing--in some way or another--his support for those answers. This is Dryden's own double strategy in the poem. He uses it to explain himself to others, as well as to try to explain things to himself. The habit of using discourse for investigation, of discovering options during the "process" of the discourse itself, reflects what we now recognize as a peculiar feature of seventeenth-century writing. In this sense, *Religio Laici* might very well be considered a kind of "self-consuming artifact."[16]

We can examine this crossing-out process by following the general progression of Dryden's own debates with his adversaries. First he offers an answer to the Deists, for instance, by insisting that *"one Sacred Book"* can provide us with "the Cure":

> If then *Heaven's Will* must needs be understood,
> (Which must, if we want *Cure*, and *Heaven* be *Good*)
> Let all Records of *Will reveal'd* be shown;
> With *Scripture*, all in equal ballance thrown,
> And *our one Sacred Book* will be *That one*.
>
> (ll. 121-25)

The "Book," Dryden goes on to say, has constantly been proven true. It provides us with the balance we have been seeking; it is "that Sacred Volume" which is "Sufficient" and "clear" (ll. 166-67). Yet when the discussion shifts focus to Father Simon's treatise, Dryden willingly agrees with the priest that Scripture is not reliable, carefully expressing this agreement in a series of conditional clauses which he will finally use to undercut Simon's own answer:

> If *Scripture*, though deriv'd from *heav'nly birth*,
> Has been but carelesly preserv'd on *Earth*;
> If *God's own People* ...
> . . . .
>   did neither *Time*, nor *Study* spare
> To keep this Book *untainted, unperplext;*
> Let in gross *Errours* to corrupt the *Text:*
> . . . .
> If *written words* from time are not secur'd,
> How can we think have *oral Sounds* endur'd?
>
> (ll. 258-71)

Dryden's final conditional clauses not only "prove" yet another argument--later to be questioned also--but nicely summarize the matter by drawing again on the exchange metaphor:

> if *one* Mouth has fail'd,
> *Immortal Lyes* on *Ages* are intail'd:

> And that some such have been, is prov'd too plain;
> If we consider *Interest, Church,* and *Gain.*
>
> (ll. 272-75)

What Dryden has argued thus far is that we cannot trust Reason, but must instead trust Scripture. That seems to be one answer. But he goes on to subvert his own cause, agreeing with Father Simon that we cannot in fact trust Scripture either--erasing one answer. He then goes on to suggest that we can neither trust church tradition--another answer cancelled before it is even fully suggested. The argument continues: if we cannot trust tradition, what can we trust?

Here Dryden pulls back even further. Faced with these two unsatisfactory options--the *"Testaments"* and the *"Creed"* (l. 283)-- he opts for a safer, more cautious position:

> More Safe, and much more modest 'tis, to say
> *God wou'd not leave Mankind without a way:*
> And that the *Scriptures,* though not *every where*
> Free from Corruption, or intire, or clear,
> Are uncorrupt, sufficient, clear, intire,
> In *all* things which our needfull *Faith* require.
>
> (ll. 295-300)

Dryden has surely stepped back from his earlier unqualified endorsement of Scripture. But he will withdraw his arguments even more as Father Simon continues to object on behalf of church tradition. Through the priest, Dryden now proposes a dual consideration--how to answer apparently contradictory arguments that hold, on the one hand, "That *Christ* is *GOD*" and, on the other, that "he's but *MAN*":

> Now what Appeal can end th' important Suit?
> *Both* parts *talk* loudly, but the *Rule* is *mute.*
>
> (ll. 312-15)

The proposition, it seems to me, evidences the way Dryden typically works his way into a consideration of dual structures. Earlier in the poem, he had described both Scripture and God as "one," yet the dual thrusts within his arguments are combatting the notion of oneness. And Dryden's own answer to this specific double-edged question indicates all the more his frustration with the arguments. Indeed, the answers, from this point on in the poem, will become less specific to the questions, and more generally revealing of Dryden's incapacity to answer the arguments. They finally become revealing of his contentment with not being able to provide answers.

Confronted, for instance, with *"Both* parts" of Simon's question, Dryden has this to say:

> Shall I speak plain, and in a Nation free
> Assume an honest *Layman's Liberty?*
> I think (according to my little Skill,)
> (To my own Mother-Church submitting still)
> That many have been sav'd, and many may,
> Who never heard this Question brought in play.
>
> (ll. 316-21)

Instead of answering the question, Dryden dismisses it. More importantly, he dismisses it at the very moment that he assumes the voice of the layman. It is not for the layman to decide between "this, or that" (l. 329). We begin to see here Dryden's sense of satisfaction with his religious dualities: he does not have to settle them; he does not have to provide us with answers. Atkins has made much of the idea that *Religio Laici* is fundamentally concerned with the "layman's" religion. Everything in both the poem and in Dryden's "Preface" surely points to such a conclusion. We can sense everywhere Dryden's discontent with the various religious "systems," and it should not therefore be surprising that Dryden's layman is content not to partake in controversial religious discourse. But Dryden, on the other hand, did so obviously want to partake in that controversy. In fact, he only assumes the role of the layman when he is unable to settle the questions in dispute. And he does just that at two pivotal points in the poem. The first instance, as we have seen, is when he had to confront "both parts" of Father Simon's question about the dual nature of God. Speaking then as an "honest Layman," he could easily dismiss the entire question. The second instance is when he must conclude his poem. Here, too, he will dismiss the argument. In a sense, Dryden has assumed two very different roles in *Religio Laici*. On the one hand, he eagerly engages himself in religious debate; on the other, he backs out of the entire controversy.

It has become conventional to say that Dryden's final position in *Religio Laici* is that of the "Anglican *via media*" or the "Horation *via media*."[17] In other words, when faced with dual extremes of one sort or another, he settles for the middle position--somewhere in between the two extremes. But that opinion presupposes that Dryden did in fact reach some conclusion, however strong or tenuous it might have been. I think that he did not. There is nothing in the final two verse paragraphs of the poem which indicates any sense of conclusion about the arguments which have been debated in the poem. Of course, Dryden is remarkably balanced in his final observations and suggestions, but it is the kind of balance that comes from a crossing-out process rather than reconciliation attempt:

> What then remains, but, waving each Extreme,
> The Tides of Ignorance, and Pride to stem:

Neither so rich a Treasure to forgo;
Nor proudly seek beyond our pow'r to know?

(ll. 427-30)

Dryden is obviously telling us what not to do, but is conspicuously avoiding any positive statement, any advice about what we should do or believe. His heavy reliance on negatives underscores the crossing-out procedure. He goes on to say, for instance, what faith is "not built on," and that it is "not likely *we* shou'd higher Soar / In search of Heav'n" (ll. 431, 437-38). Moreover, couplets often turn on the meaning of previous couplets, first establishing a point of argument, then dismissing the implications of that argument:

Faith is not built on disquisitions vain;
The things we *must* believe, are *few*, and *plain:*
But since men *will* believe more than they *need;*
And every man will make *himself* a Creed....

(ll. 431-34)

In "waving each extreme," Dryden is cancelling each extreme: we cannot do this, so we must do that, but since we cannot do that, we must do the other. This self-generating procedure continues, until there is no other point of reference to settle the matter. It is as if Dryden backed himself into a corner of the checkerboard where the players are locked in a stalemate position, with no other option than to slide back and forth.

The poem ends with the layman's voice--a voice not of argumentation, nor of reconciliation, but of dismissal:

'Tis some Relief, that points not clearly known,
Without much hazard may be let alone:
. . . .
For points obscure are of small use to learn:
But *Common quiet* is *Mankind's concern.*

(ll. 443-44, 449-50)

Dryden has not made his "own Opinions clear" so much as he has cleared away his opinions. Since he has taken no solid position, it seems only appropriate that he should, once again relying on negatives, "neither Praise expect, nor Censure fear" (ll. 451-52). And there is yet another, final, kind of dismissal in the poem, the drastic shift in tone that merges subject *("Sacred Truth")* with style *("Tom Sternhold's*, or *Tom Sha---ll's Rhimes")* (ll. 455-56). But the merger itself is incongruous, at once dismissing the serious quality of the subject and ridiculous quality of the style. It is, in fact, much like the unbalanced contracts associated with each religious system--indicating a severe discontinuity between "Means" and "Effects."

Religio Laici is a poem built upon two-sided arguments and their ensuing dismissals: first Deistic bargains, then clerical bargains, and finally individual scriptural bargains. It is also built upon Dryden's own double strategy--his own bargaining with each religious position that he ponders, and finally his dismissal of a series of conflicts that prove too complex to synthesize.

Let me conclude by returning to my initial assumption--that Dryden was not a profound religious poet. There is every reason to appreciate, I think, the poetic value of what Dryden was *not* in his religious poetry. For if we do not find in his poetry the torment of faith and doubt, we do discover just the opposite--a poet capable of dancing around religious issues, carefully making his way through their contradictions, and ultimately content with his own nimbleness and dexterity. The best part of argument, after all, was dexterity. It was also the best part of satire--as Dryden himself reminded us when describing his portrayal of Zimri in *Absalom and Achitophel.* If Dryden is the master politician in that poem-- largely because of his dualistic vision--then he ultimately becomes the contented layman in *Religio Laici.* He is enraptured with the religious whirlwind about him, but gracefully bows out when it comes time to take a position.

Afterword: Dividing the Crown

The image of the circle which recurs throughout *All For Love* also presents itself during the grand chorus of *Alexander's Feast*. Just as Dryden had used that image to encapsulate the world of the lovers in his drama--with rings of contract and wreaths of victory, so he relies on a similar circular image--the crown--to encapsulate the world of the musicians in his ode. But, somewhat unsure as to who should receive that crown of victory, Dryden thinks twice about the matter, finally deciding to divide the circle: "Let old *Timotheus* yield the Prize, / Or both divide the Crown." When we consider the different accomplishments of the two musicians--Timotheus and Cecilia--it does seem only fair that the crown be divided. The two musical actions are, after all, diametrically opposed: Timotheus "rais'd a Mortal to the Skies," Cecilia "drew an Angel down."

Perhaps the division of the crown was a compromise measure. Perhaps--despite the fact that Dryden was supposed to be writing the ode in honor of St. Cecilia--he could not quite bring himself to allow Timotheus to "yield the Prize," and thus settled on both musicians sharing the victory. Such a view would clearly be in line with our favorite critical sentiments about Dryden: he balances issues, reaches some sense of equilibrium, reflects a *via media*, holds to the classical mean.

But such balance, I think, does not at all describe what actually happens in *Alexander's Feast*. Johnson, for one, obviously felt this way when he censured the ending of the ode: "The conclusion is vicious; the musick of Timotheus, which 'raised a mortal to the skies,' had only a metaphorical power; that of Cecilia, which 'drew an angel down,' had a real effect; the crown therefore could not reasonably be divided."[1] If Johnson's description of the conclusion as vicious and unreasonable sounds harsh, we can at least say that it indicates how strongly he sensed the double thrusts at the ode's ending. There is the opposition of two forms of music (sensual and heavenly), of two master musicians (Timotheus and Cecilia), of two musical effects (metaphorical and real), and of two crisscross movements (rise and descent).

But these dual thrusts are what we continually encounter in Dryden. Nor was this the first time that Johnson found fault with one of Dryden's "doublings."[2] Particularly the juxtaposed upward and downward motion, the crossing of two musicians, should remind us of the reflexive structure of *All For Love*. There the action hinges on the dual "fate" of each character, a fate which is both the pursuer and the pursued--meeting characters "at each double." There, too, the circle of the world is divided, not only into the opposing camps of Egypt and Rome, but into the real and the metaphorical--the world that is really lost, and the love that is metaphorically won. Various commentators, in fact, have seen what Johnson described as the opposition of metaphorical and real in *Alexander's Feast* to be a pivotal issue in *All For Love*. Hughes speaks of the lovers' dilemma in terms of "the contrast between actual mortality and imagined divinity," and Alan Fisher describes Antony and Cleopatra as "king and queen not of the real world but of the world of the mind."[3] And not surprisingly, Johnson himself found Dryden's drama to contain a "moral" fault very similar to the one he detected in *Alexander's Feast:* the play seemed to award the victory to the lovers when the crown clearly belonged to Rome.[4] As in *Alexander's Feast*, the crown in *All For Love* is notably divided. Conquests become defeats, and defeats turn into victories. In this world of divisions and oppositions, it is difficult to say who wins and who loses.

To a large extent that difficulty arises from differences of perspective. And that problem of perspective is one which Dryden aptly summarized in his prefatory comments to *Absalom and Achitophel:* "And every man is a Knave or an Ass to the contrary side."[5] Of course we are given a "Party Poem," a satire admittedly slanted in favor of one side. But even in that one-sided story Dryden finds it easy to award praise and censure, to "Tickle" and "Hurt," at the same time.

Again, reference to *Alexander's Feast* can help highlight Dryden's dual concerns, here with reference to his political poem. We might, for instance, compare David's world of stability to the staid demeanor of Cecilia's music. Both are asserted at the end of each poem, and both--as several critics agree--are somewhat out of tune with the livelier and brisker atmosphere established by Dryden earlier in each poem. Similarly, we can compare Achitophel's world of rebellion to the violent changes in passion excited by Timotheus. Just as Achitophel lures Absalom into rebellious action, so Timotheus entices Alexander into various states of turmoil. Dryden seems to award the victory in *Absalom and Achitophel* to David, just as he seems to crown Cecilia at the end of his ode. But the opposites of David and Cecilia have already strongly asserted themselves: we have already witnessed the storms of political rebellion and the frenzied emotions excited by music. The crown seems just as divided in both poems, though for obvious political reasons Dryden could not make the division so clear-cut in *Absalom and Achitophel.* Perhaps we might draw on the opposition of real and metaphorical to describe the divisions here. David, from this perspective, must win the real crown (as Caesar and Rome must win the world, as Cecilia must replace Timotheus). But the pictures Dryden gives us in his political poem--of the profligate Charles, the wavering Buckingham, the scheming Shaftesbury--enjoy a victory all their own. Metaphorically, the crown may be theirs, too.

Though there is no real or metaphorical crown in *Religio Laici*, the discourse is clearly split in both its structure and points of argument. We encounter crossings in various religious exchanges, and we discover a poet who seems content with the way "extremes" cancel each other. But again, we have seen these crossings and exchanges before. In *Religio Laici* they nonetheless take on a peculiar function, perhaps because of the complex nature of the arguments in the poem. As Dryden searches for a way out of the labyrinth of argument which forms the substance of his verse essay, he seems to become less interested in the need to award any crown at all. When opposed opinions and arguments cancel each other, we are left not with vying options, but with no options. And that situation, at least in *Religio Laici*, seems rather appealing to Dryden. When, at the end of the poem, we see him settling for "Common quiet," we see a poet undisturbed by the flux and oppositions which surround him.

Dryden's position at the end of his religious discourse resembles the perspective he assumed at the end of *Alexander's Feast:* here he presents another kind of crossing--the ascent of a mortal, the descent of an angel. We might even say that Dryden's final poetic perspective, his attitude at the end of poems, often reflects a curious kind of acknowledgement and consent, a willing submission to the way things have turned out. In *Religio Laici* we hear him admitting, "'Tis some Relief, that points not clearly known, / Without much hazard may be let alone." It is that sense of admission evoked by the word "let" that we hear again at the end of the ode: "Let old *Timotheus* yield the Prize, / Or both divide the Crown."

The crisscross patterns, the exchanges, the doublings and divisions all account for the liveliness we find in Dryden's work. His dramatic and poetic worlds are always characterized by flux--movements in different, often opposed, directions. It was a kind of movement very similar to the concepts of motion that, as we have seen, figure so strongly in the writings of Montaigne, Bacon, and Hobbes.[6] We might also recall that it was Alexander the Great who epitomized for Montaigne the man of action. Surely he did for Dryden as well, but for Dryden, Alexander was also the man of oppositions: he is the "Brave" who deserves the "Fair," he is the "present Deity," the "vanquish'd Victor," the conquerer who enjoys "Pleasure" and "Pain."[7] But what we see in Alexander are also the contrary forces in Dryden--the paradoxes, contradictions, and oppositions that his own muse dictated, that consumed his poetic vision.

I have suggested earlier that Alexander's feast was also Dryden's feast--the feast of duelling forces. But there is a certain risk involved in making such a suggestion: Dryden, at least in terms of our conventional assumptions about him, should not be aligned with Alexander at all. For one thing, Alexander is controlled by the dictates of Timotheus, rather than himself controlling his actions. For another, Dryden should conventionally, perhaps even morally,[8] be associated with Cecilia who inspires notes of "holy Love." The problem, however, is that in *Alexander's Feast*, as well as in his other great works, there was a marked difference between what Dryden should have been doing and what he actually did. Like Cecilia's music, Dryden's art should have served "To mend the Choires above." Instead, it served the exact opposite purpose.

When Alexander, for instance, is lured by Timotheus to turn his actions from war to love, Dryden describes the result in this way:

> The Many rend the Skies, with loud Applause;
> So Love was Crown'd, but Musique won the Cause.

The opposition of "mend" and "rend" neatly summarizes Dryden's predicament. The ideal striving for synthesis was continually subverted in him by his preoccupation, at times fascination, with division. Dryden, like Shakespeare, must have been consumed with what Rabkin called "a perennial sense of conflict between human ideals at any moment in time."[9] That is why, like the "half-man" figure of Alexas in *All For Love*, he was never entirely true to his ideals. Caught within a circle of his own devising, Dryden was pursued by a poetic fate which demanded a single vision. But he himself pursued an entirely different fate, one which supplied him with the conflict and opposition so natural to his poetic temperament. Those double fates help explain why Dryden was himself so often at odds with what he was supposed to be writing, and why the very crown of his own poetic achievement was also divided.

In a letter to his publisher Tonson, Dryden had this to say about *Alexander's Feast:* "I am glad to heare from all Hands, that my Ode is esteemd the best of all my poetry, by all the Town: I thought so my self when I writ it...."[10] On a different occasion, which Dryden's early biographer Malone describes, a young man "congratulated Dryden on having produced the noblest Ode that had ever been written in any language. 'You are right, young gentleman,' [Dryden] replied, 'a nobler Ode never was produced, nor ever will.' "[11] The satisfaction that Dryden felt about the ode shows us a poet who, like Alexander, followed the dictates of his muse and enjoyed the feast of his art. If that feast was the feast of oppositions, then we can feel certain that Dryden considered it the best part of his literary expression.

NOTES

NOTES TO CHAPTER 1

1 Dryden was elected to the Royal Society on Charleton's nomination. Early poems which Dryden wrote on the restoration of Charles II include "Astraea Redux" (1660), "To His Sacred Majesty" (1661), and "To My Lord Chancellor" (1662, directly addressed to Edward Hyde, Earl of Clarendon, and on several occasions indirectly to Charles himself).

2 The two views are from, respectively, Earl R. Wasserman, "Dryden's Epistle to Charleton," *JEGP*, 55 (1956), 201-12, and Phillip Harth, *Contexts of Dryden's Thought* (Chicago: Univ. of Chicago Press, 1968), pp. 21-25. Harth conveniently summarizes Wasserman's views in his analysis.

3 *Lives of the English Poets*, ed. G.B. Hill (1905; rpt. New York: Ocatagon Books, 1967), I, 459.

4 *The Life of John Dryden* (1834; rpt. Lincoln: Univ. of Nebraska Press, 1963), p. 260.

5 *Dryden* (1888; rpt. New York: AMS Press, 1968), p. 103.

6 *John Dryden: Some Biographical Facts and Problems* (1940; rpt. Gainesville: Univ. of Florida Press, 1965), p. 129.

7 Scott, p. 32.

8 "A Discourse Concerning the Original and Progress of Satire," in *Works*, IV, 59. Also see *Dryden: The Critical Heritage*, ed. James Kinsley and Helen Kinsley (New York: Barnes and Noble, 1971), pp. 10-11.

9 "Dryden," in *General Dictionary, Historical and Critical*, (n.p.: n.p., 1734-41), IV, 687.

10 James Osborn provides a summary of the accounts of Birch, Derrick, and particularly Malone, *John Dryden: Some Biographical Facts and Problems*, pp. 3-71. The statement of Derrick's which I quote can be found in Osborn, p. 17. For some of Malone's comments on the attacks made against Dryden, see *An Account of the Life and Writings of the Author* in *The Critical and Miscellaneous Prose Works of John Dryden* (London: H. Baldwin and Sons, 1800), pp. 541-42.

11 Johnson, p. 334.

12 Johnson, p. 377.

13 Scott, pp. 1-2.

14 Scott, pp. 2, 428.

15 Saintsbury, p. 103.

16 Saintsbury, p. 79.

17 Osborn, p. 100.

18 *The Life of John Dryden* (Chapel Hill: Univ. of North Carolina Press, 1961), p. 175.

[19] Ward, p. 222.

[20] "Dryden's 'Unideal Vacancy,' " ECS, 12 (1978), 74.

[21] Love, p. 88.

[22] John Dryden: A Study of His Poetry (1920; rpt. Bloomington: Indiana Univ. Press, 1960), p. 68.

[23] The labels I use are selections from our main body of Dryden criticism: Bernard Schilling, Dryden and the Conservative Myth (New Haven: Yale Univ. Press, 1961); Alan Roper, Dryden's Poetic Kingdoms (New York: Barnes and Noble, 1965); Louis I. Bredvold, The Intellectual Milieu of John Dryden (Ann Arbor: Univ. of Michigan Press, 1934); Phillip Harth, Contexts of Dryden's Thought; James D. Garrison, Dryden and the Tradition of Panegyric (Berkeley: Univ. of California Press, 1975); W.K. Thomas, The Crafting of "Absalom and Achitophel" (Waterloo: Wilfred Laurier Univ. Press, 1978); Arthur Hoffman, John Dryden's Imagery (Gainesville: Univ. of Florida Press, 1962).

[24] The Art of John Dryden (Lexington: Univ. of Kentucky Press, 1969), p. 103.

[25] SP, 72 (1975), 348-66.

[26] 2nd ed. (Great Britain: New Directions, 1947). Empson's analysis is quite brief. See pp. 74-77.

[27] Seven Types of Ambiguity, p. 74.

[28] Following Empson's obervations, I have offered some further analysis of Dryden's word order in my article "Dryden's Ambiguous Syntax," Forum, 16 (1978), 7-11. Also see Allan Rodway, "By Algebra to Augustanism," in Essays on Style and Language, ed. Roger Fowler (London: Routledge and Kegan Paul, 1966), pp. 63-66, and J. Douglas Canfield, "Anarchy and Style: What Dryden 'Grants' in Absalom and Achitophel," PLL, 14 (1978), 83-87.

[29] (London: Cambridge Univ. Press, 1975), p. 70. For an explication of Pechter's argument, I draw mainly from his initial chapter, "The Structure of Dryden's Theory," pp. 11-35. I should point out that Pechter shuns the term "duality" and uses instead the word "doubleness," believing that "duality" connotes "a thoroughgoing ontology" which he considers uncharacteristic of Dryden's thought (p. 14).

[30] John Dryden II, Papers Read at Clark Library Seminars, 1974; pub. William Andrews Clark Memorial Library (Los Angeles: Univ. of Calif., 1978), p. 12. Interestingly, one of the oppositions that Marion Bodwell Smith finds characteristic of Shakespeare involves "contrasts in tone and mingling of genres," oppositions very similar to the kind of "discontinuity" that Ehrenpreis finds characteristic of Dryden. See Dualities in Shakespeare (Toronto: Univ. of Toronto Press, 1966), p. 17.

[31] "Continuity and Coruscation," pp. 19 and 21. Ehrenpreis's discussion of "Dryden the Dramatist" in his recent Acts of Implication (Berkeley: Univ. of Calif. Press, 1980) also addresses some of the issues presented in his Clark Lecture. See especially pp. 24-26.

[32] Love, pp. 80-81.

[33] Love, p. 88.

[34] After I completed this manuscript, Laura Brown's article on "The Ideology of Restoration Poetic Form: John Dryden" appeared in PMLA, 97 (1982), 395-407. Her discovery of "disjunction" in Dryden's poetry clearly has some

affinities with my perception of his "dualities," and I happily cite her as yet
another critic who offers a revisionist reading of Dryden. Perhaps our
arguments differ most on the matter of Dryden's poetic intentions and
temperament. Brown sees Dryden's form as continually subverting its claims:
"It proposes perfect equivalence, but it produces only disjunction. In this
respect, Dryden's poetic form is the opposite of expansive, generous, or open.
In fact, it can more accurately be described as blind...." I would argue that
Dryden's expansiveness and generosity have always been his most appealing
qualities. His great literary biographers have consistently noted these qualities
about him.

[35] See John Hollander, *The Untuning of the Sky* (Princeton: Princeton Univ.
Press, 1961), especially for a discussion of the employment of the Cecilia theme
in the late seventeenth century, pp. 258-79.

[36] Notably, J. Buck, "The Ascetic's Banquet: The Morality of *Alexander's Feast*,"
TSLL, 17 (1975), 573-89, and Ruth Smith, "The Argument and Contexts of
Dryden's *Alexander's Feast*," *SEL*, 18 (1978), 465-90.

[37] See Ehrenpreis, note 30 above. Van Doren, *John Dryden: A Study of His
Poetry*, p. 206.

[38] Smith, p. 468, n. 4.

NOTES TO CHAPTER 2

[1] One of the fullest discussions of this preoccupation can be found in Robert
Grudin's *Mighty Opposites: Shakespeare and Renaissance Contrariety*
(Berkeley: Univ. of Calif. Press, 1979), pp. 13-50. Martin Price, *To the Palace of
Wisdom: Studies in Order and Energy from Dryden to Blake* (New York:
Doubleday, 1964), bases his study of "dialectical excess" in Restoration and
eighteenth- century literature on Pascal's central theme--the "double nature of
man" (p. 19).

[2] I am drawing on the pivotal discussions of Louis I. Bredvold, *The Intellectual
Milieu of John Dryden*, pp. 16-46, and Phillip Harth, *Contexts of Dryden's
Thought*, pp. 1-31.

[3] *The Intellectual Milieu*, p. 41.

[4] *Contexts of Dryden's Thought*, pp. 20-21.

[5] See Virgil K. Whitaker, "Francis Bacon's Intellectual Milieu," Paper Read at
Clark Library, 1961; rpt. in *Essential Articles for the Study of Francis Bacon*,
ed. Brian Vickers (Hamden: Archon, 1968), pp. 28-50.

[6] Suggested by Pierre Villey, *Montaigne et Francois Bacon* (Paris, 1913), pp. 38-
39. The influence of Montaigne on Bacon was at one time so readily
acknowledged that Saintsbury disparagingly referred to it as "that Montaigne-
Bacon craze" (see his introduction to *The Essays of Montaigne*, note 7 below,
p. x). Jacob Zeitlein, "The Development of Bacon's Essays--With Special
Reference to the Question of Montaigne's Influence Upon Them," *JEGP*, 27
(1928), 496-519, rightly questions the direct influence of Montaigne on Bacon,
emphasizing the difference between Montaigne's profound skepticism and
Bacon's belief in the potential of science. But he admits, as Villey originally
noted and most would agree, that both essayists shared a lively spirit of

inquiry. Robert Grudin's remarks on the two figures are also relevant, *Mighty Opposites*, p. 46, n. 7.

7 *The Essays of Montaigne*, trans. John Florio (1632; rpt. London: David Nutt, 1892), III, 166. I refer throughout to Florio's translation by volume and page number. Although Dryden will often quote Montaigne in the original French, the Florio translation was the most popular of the day.

8 Barbara C. Bowen, *The Age of Bluff: Paradox and Ambiguity in Rabelais & Montaigne*, Illinois Studies in Language and Literature, 62 (Urbana: Univ. of Illinois Press, 1972), pp. 126-27.

9 See Wiley, "Francis Bacon: Induction and/or Rhetoric," *SLI*, 4 (1971), 72; and Fish, *Self-Consuming Artifacts* (Berkeley: Univ. of Calif. Press, 1972), pp. 78-155.

10 *The Works of Francis Bacon*, ed. James Spedding, R.L. Ellis, and D.D. Heath (Boston: Brown and Taggard, 1861), pp. 83-84. All references are to the *Works*, vol. 12 for the *Essays*, vol. 1 for *Novum Organum*.

11 Whitaker suggests several traditions that Bacon was following in his division and systemization of analysis. See "Francis Bacon's Intellectual Milieu," pp. 31-39.

12 *Self-Consuming Artifacts*, p. 124.

13 See Wiley, pp. 72 and 77.

14 *History of the Royal Society* (1667; rpt. St. Louis: Washington Univ. Studies, 1958), p. 104.

15 Harth discusses the influence of Bacon's reformed skepticism on several leading scientists of the day. Interestingly, the two members of the Royal Society who are quoted by Harth specifically address themselves to the importance of dual and contrary notions in the scientific method. Joseph Glanvill in his *Plus Ultra* writes that the scientist "never concludes but upon resolution to alter his mind upon contrary evidence ... with great [deference] to *opposite* Perswaision, candour to *dissenters*, and *calmness* in *contradictions*...." And Robert Boyle in *The Sceptical Chymist* insists that he seeks the "undoubted truth" through two procedures: "though if I miss it in one opinion, I proceed to search after it in the opposite...." See *Contexts of Dryden's Thought*, pp. 9-11.

16 Sprat, p. 104.

17 *Opticks: Or, a Treatise of the Reflections, Refractions, Inflections and Colours of Light*, rpt. from the 4th edition, London, 1730 (New York: Dover Publications, 1952), Part I, p. 1. Subsequent citations are to this edition and are noted by page number.

18 See, for instance, Marjorie Hope Nicolson's comments on how Newton embraced the corpuscular theory "with evident hesitation," *Newton Demands the Muse* (Princeton: Princeton Univ. Press, 1946), pp. 64-65.

19 See Cohen's "Preface" in the Dover edition of the *Opticks*, p. ix.

20 *Shakespeare and the Common Understanding* (New York: The Free Press, 1967), pp. 13-26. Other major studies in this area include Rosalie Colie, *Paradoxia Epidemica* (Princeton: Princeton Univ. Press, 1966); Smith, *Dualities in Shakespeare* (1966); Harriet Hawkins, *Likeness of Truth in Elizabethan and Restoration Drama* (Oxford: Clarendon Press, 1972); Grudin, *Mighty Opposites* (1979).

21 *Gulliver's Travels,* ed. Herbert Davis (Oxford: Basil Blackwell, 1965), p. 163.

22 For the texts and discussion of the different versions of Newton's *Scholium,* see *Isaac Newton's Principia,* ed. Alexandre Koyne and I. Bernard Cohen (Cambridge, Mass.: Harvard Univ. Press, 1971), pp. 140-45.

23 Quoted in *Isaac Newton's Principia,* p. 245.

24 The illustration appeared in each of the three editions of *Leviathan* which were dated 1651. For a full discussion of the editions, and of other "ornaments" which appeared on the title pages of editions which were obviously printed after that date, see Hugh MacDonald and Mary Hargreaves, *Thomas Hobbes: A Bibliography* (London: The Bibliographical Society, 1952), pp. 27 ff.

25 *Leviathan, Or the Matter, Forme and Power of a Commonwealth Ecclesiasticall and Civil,* ed. Michael Oakeshott (Oxford: Basil Blackwell, 1946), p. 31. Further citations are to this edition and are noted by page number.

26 *The Anatomy Of Leviathan* (London: Macmillan, 1968), p. 64. McNeilly's conclusion about the existence of different phenomena in Hobbes's philosophy is in line with several of my observations about the dual nature of his discourse. "If Hobbes's arguments are valid, then, violence is not a product merely, or even chiefly, of disreputable human passions.... It arises, on the contrary, from the relations between rational beings who have values, but not necessarily the same values. Hence there is no question whether violence should be accepted or rejected, but only how best its employment can be regulated" (p. 254). It is not the negation of differences and oppositions that validates Hobbes's philosophy, but their regulation. Also see S. Morris Engel, "Analogy and Equivocation in Hobbes," *Philosophy,* 37 (1962), 326-55, who argues that there is "a certain inner struggle of mind" in Hobbes. Though Reason is Hobbes's "principle of synthesis," his arguments rest on " 'false' analogies" and "a series of minor equivocations" which make that synthesis untenable.

27 The influence of Montaigne on Dryden, for instance, is a highly debated issue. See especially Harth's discussion of this subject, *Contexts of Dryden's Thought,* pp. 1-31. And the influence of Hobbesian ideas on Dryden has been discussed at length and from a variety of perspectives. See, for example, Mildred E. Hartsock, "Dryden's Plays: A Study in Ideas," in *Seventeenth Century Studies,* 2nd series, ed. Robert Shafer (Princeton: Princeton Univ. Press, 1937), pp. 69-176; John A. Winterbottom, "The Place of Hobbesian Ideas in Dryden's Tragedies," *JEGP,* 57 (1958), 665-83; Thomas Fujimura, "The Appeal of Dryden's Heroic Plays," *PMLA,* 75 (1960), 37-45. Alan S. Fisher, "Daring to be Absurd: The Paradoxes of *The Conquest of Granada,*" *SP,* 73 (1976), 414-39, observes the interesting example of Almanzor who can both rely on Hobbes for a maxim, and then "can turn Hobbes around" (p. 422). One might say that Dryden is being paradoxical and dualistic in his very use of Hobbes.

NOTES TO CHAPTER 3

1 *The Rambler,* No. 31, July 3, 1750; conveniently reprinted in *Dryden: The Critical Heritage,* ed. James Kinsley and Helen Kinsley, pp. 312-13.

2 See Kinsley's note, *Dryden: The Critical Heritage,* p. 312, n. 2.

[3] *Life of Dryden,* p. 361.

[4] See Everett H. Emerson, Harold E. Davis, and Ira Johnson, "Intention and Achievement in *All For Love,*" *CE,* 17 (1955), 84-87, who make much of Johnson's comments and suggest that "the play is full of confusions" (p. 87). Also see Bruce King, "Dryden's Intent in *All For Love,*" *CE,* 24 (1963), 267-71, who challenges that view and offers some explanations for the apparent incongruity in the play.

[5] Waith, *The Herculean Hero in Marlowe, Chapman, Shakespeare and Dryden* (New York: Columbia Univ. Press, 1962); Miner, *Dryden's Poetry,* pp. 36-73; Hughes, "The Significance of *All For Love,*" *ELH,* 37 (1970), 540-63; Kearful, " ' 'Tis Past Recovery': Tragic Consciousness in *All For Love,*" *MLQ,* 34 (1973), 227-46; and Canfield, "The Jewel of Great Price: Mutability and Constancy in Dryden's *All For Love,*" *ELH,* 42 (1974), 38-61.

[6] Miner, p. 73.

[7] Hughes, pp. 561-62.

[8] Much of the criticism on *All For Love* comments, in some fashion or another, on Dryden's use of Shakespeare. For the purposes of my own argument, I would suggest that Dryden not only followed but indeed inherited Shakespeare's own divided "complementary" vision. Norman Rabkin discusses such a vision in *Antony and Cleopatra (Shakespeare and the Common Understanding,* pp. 185-88). For other examinations of Shakespeare's play from this perspective, see Smith, *Dualities in Shakespeare,* pp. 189-214, and Grudin, *Mighty Opposites,* pp. 165-79.

[9] *Shakespeare and the Common Understanding,* p. 188. Though I quote Rabkin to offer indirect support for my argument about Dryden, I was nonetheless disappointed to read Rabkin's comparison of Shakespeare's *Antony and Cleopatra* and Dryden's *All For Love* in his recent book *Shakespeare and the Problem of Meaning* (Chicago: Univ. of Chicago Press, 1981), pp. 64-72. He argues that whereas "Shakespeare makes it impossible for anyone who responds fully to feel certain that Antony ought to reject his splendid mistress" or that he ought to renounce "his obligation to the austere idealism of Rome," Dryden "never for a moment leaves us in doubt as to how to judge the action" (p. 67). My argument obviously questions this distinction between the two authors, and assumes that Dryden is just as equivocal as his predecessor.

[10] *Acts of Implication,* p. 46. Ehrenpreis's recent study of Dryden's drama often calls attention to "paradoxes," "turnabouts," "Intellectual duels," and "polarities" that were so much a part of Dryden's dramatic practice (pp. 23-25).

[11] "Daring to be Absurd," p. 436.

[12] So observes Miner: "Antony had tried to be emperor at the courts of both arms and love.... The play shows that it is impossible to sustain such a life" (p. 63). But though Miner sees "love and arms" as irreconcilable, he suggests that some final union is achieved through the merger of "love and death" at the end of the play (p. 73).

[13] See the discussion of Hobbes in Chapter 2.

[14] Miner, pp. 41-42. Also see Hughes, "The Significance of *All For Love,*" pp. 542-43.

[15] "Necessity and the Winter: The Tragedy of *All For Love,*" pp. 198-99.

[16] "Dryden and the Analysis of Shakespeare's Techniques," *RES*, 19 (1943), 179, 170.

[17] Miner, p. 54. Howard Weinbrot, "Alexas in *All For Love:* His Genealogy and Function," *SP*, 64 (1967), 625-39, offers the fullest critical discussion of Alexas, though I would disagree with his interpretation of Alexas's function as the workings of evil in the play.

[18] Canfield, "The Jewel of Great Price: Mutability and Constancy in *All For Love*," sees the imagery of jewelry as reflective of Cleopatra's "constancy." I view the image differently. Its circularity and the conflicting implications of that circularity complement the opposition of union and division. Particularly the circularity of bribery, which is what the jewels are often used for, is something we will run into again in *Religio Laici*. See the discussion of this matter in Chapter 5.

[19] *The Breaking of the Circle* (New York: Columbia Univ. Press, 1960), pp. 7-8. Interestingly, Nicolson also observes that for Bacon, too, the Circle of Perfection was "a mere fiction" (p. 9).

[20] "The Rhetoric of Temporality," in *Interpretation: Theory and Practice*, ed. C.S. Singleton (Baltimore: Johns Hopkins Univ. Press, 1969), pp. 192, 202, 198. The application of de Man's theory to *All For Love* is my own.

NOTES TO CHAPTER 4

[1] J.R. Jones, "Introduction," *The Restored Monarchy, 1660-1688*, ed. J.R. Jones (London: Macmillan, 1979), p. 22. We might also look to the poem's main villain, Shaftesbury, for a similar case of personal inconsistency. See Jones's comments, "Parties and Parliament," p. 60.

[2] Quoted by Miller in "The Later Stuart Monarchy," in *The Restored Monarchy*, ed. Jones, p. 38.

[3] "A Discourse Concerning the Original and Progress of Satire," in *Works*, IV, 71.

[4] "The Original and Progress of Satire," IV, 71.

[5] *Dryden and the Conservative Myth*, p. 277.

[6] Schilling, p. 148; Miner, *Dryden's Poetry*, p. 119.

[7] Jack, *Augustan Satire: Intention and Idiom in English Poetry, 1660-1750* (Oxford: Clarendon, 1952), p. 75; Zwicker, *Dryden's Political Poetry: The Typology of King and Nation* (Providence: Brown Univ. Press, 1972), p. 88; Emslie, "Dryden's Couplets: Wit and Conversation," *EC*, 11 (1961), 267.

[8] "A Reading of *Absalom and Achitophel*," *YES*, 6 (1976), 56-60.

[9] Miner, pp. 116-17.

[10] *PQ*, 57 (1978), 359-82.

[11] The best discussions of these rhetorical patterns are still to be found in Ruth Wallerstein, "The Development of the Rhetoric and Metre of the Heroic Couplet, Especially in 1625-1645," *PMLA*, 50 (1935), 166-209, and George Williamson, "The Rhetorical Pattern of Neo-Classical Wit," *MP*, 33 (1935), 55-81.

[12] Piper, *The Heroic Couplet* (Cleveland: Case Western Reserve, 1969), p. 110.

[13] Ramsey, p. 110.

[14] In *Seven Types of Ambiguity*. See my discussion of Empson's observations in Chapter 1.

[15] See Dryden's letter to an "Unidentified Person," in *The Letters of John Dryden*, ed. Charles E. Ward (Durham: Duke Univ. Press, 1942), pp. 14-16.

[16] "Literature in the Reader: Affective Stylistics," *Is There A Text in This Class?* (Cambridge: Harvard Univ. Press, 1980), p. 26.

[17] Schilling, pp. 206-7.

[18] "Dryden's Absalom," *EC*, 11 (1961), 278.

[19] Schilling, p. 162.

[20] See Ricks's review of the criticism on Absalom, "Dryden's Absalom," pp. 273-74.

NOTES TO CHAPTER 5

[1] *Men of Letters and the English Public in the Eighteenth Century* (1881; rpt. London: Kegan Paul, Trench, Trubner, 1948), p. 202.

[2] "Dryden's Apparent Scepticism," *EIC*, 20 (1970), 180.

[3] G. Douglas Atkins, *The Faith of John Dryden* (Lexington: Univ. Press of Kentucky, 1980), p. 3.

[4] Arthur Hoffman, *John Dryden's Imagery*, pp. 65-70, discusses the "oxymoron of Reason" in the poem, a topic which Sanford Budick treats in terms of the "apparent contradiction" about the meaning and function of "discourse" in *Religio Laici*. See *Dryden and the Abyss of Light* (New Haven: Yale Univ. Press, 1970), p. 21. Phillip Harth, *Contexts of Dryden's Thought*, p. 174, uses the term "paradox" to refer to the confusion over the poem's structure.

[5] Budick uses the phrase "dialectic of ideas" and identifies as well a variety of two-fold structures in *Religio Laici*, including the "two simultaneous and complementary operations" which govern the poem's progress, and the "Two Lights" of Reason and Scripture which shape Dryden's own perspective on spiritual "illumination" (pp. 93 and 120).

[6] Harth uses the term "rhetorical strategy" to account for Dryden's approaches to his subject (pp. 196-97). Atkins also speaks of a kind of rhetorical strategy at work in the poem (p. 7). The term is, of course, useful to identify any kind of design or intention that a poet might have in mind. And, I suspect, it is just as useful when describing a critic's approach.

[7] *The Intellectual Milieu of John Dryden*, pp. 73-129.

[8] Harth, see especially Chapter One, "The Sceptical Critic," and Chapter Six, "Defender of the Faith: Anglican vs. Catholic."

[9] Budick, p. 159. Other critics who have treated *Religio Laici* in terms of Anglican apologetics include Thomas H. Fujimura, "Dryden's *Religio Laici*: An Anglican Poem," *PMLA*, 76 (1961), 205-17, and Elias J. Chiasson, "Dryden's Apparent Scepticism in *Religio Laici*," *HTR*, 54 (1961), 207-21.

[10] Atkins, see especially pp. 5, 98-99, and 111-14. Specifically on *Religio Laici*, see pp. 93-95.

[11] For a very different reading of the poem, see K.W. Gransden, "What Kind of Poem is *Religio Laici?*" *SEL*, 17 (1977), 397-406, who considers the poem as a

very consistent, straightforward declaration of faith, and places it in the tradition of Roman verse satire, particularly that of Persius and Juvenal.

[12] Atkins, p. 72.

[13] Hoffman, p. 69. Also see Emslie, "Dryden's Couplets: Imagery Vowed to Poverty," *CQ,* 2 (1960), 51-57.

[14] Budick, pp. 147-50.

[15] Martin Price offers a particularly interesting interpretation of the "mercantile figures" in *The Hind and the Panther,* also seeing them in dual terms, specifically in terms of "Pascal's wager," *To the Palace of Wisdom,* pp. 72-73.

[16] I am of course referring to the critical perspective of Stanley Fish, *Self-Consuming Artifacts,* whose notion of the "dialectical presentation" seems particularly applicable to Dryden: "For the end of a dialectical experience is (or should be) nothing less than a *conversion,* not only a changing, but an exchanging of minds" (p. 2). The metaphor of exchange might well have served Dryden for this purpose.

[17] The terms are from, respectively, Harth, p. 224, and Atkins, p. 73.

NOTES TO AFTERWORD

[1] *Life of Dryden,* p. 457.

[2] See the beginning of Chapter 3 where I discuss Johnson's observations.

[3] Hughes, "The Significance of *All For Love,*" p. 563, and Fisher, "Necessity and the Winter: The Tragedy of *All For Love,*" p. 202.

[4] Johnson, p. 361.

[5] See the discussion of the preface to *Absalom and Achitophel* in Chapter 4.

[6] See the discussion of this matter in Chapter 2.

[7] The opposition of pain and pleasure, Grudin observes, goes back to Petrarch who portrayed "erotic emotion as an unresolved tension in which opposed elements like pain and pleasure or body and spirit struggle for supremacy" (*Mighty Opposites,* p. 17). This "struggle" is of course epitomized in Dryden's Alexander.

[8] See particularly Buck, "The Ascetic's Banquet: The Morality of *Alexander's Feast,*" p. 577.

[9] *Shakespeare and the Common Understanding,* p. 18.

[10] *The Letters of John Dryden,* ed. Ward, p. 98.

[11] *An Account of the Life and Writings of the Author,* p. 476.

www.ingramcontent.com/pod-product-compliance
Lightning Source LLC
Chambersburg PA
CBHW050947030426
42339CB00007B/329